Glencoe

Monarch of Glens

First published in Great Britain in 1990 by
Colin Baxter Photography Ltd.,
Unit 2/3, Block 6,
Caldwellside Industrial Estate,
LANARK, ML11 6SR

British Library Cataloguing in Publication Data
Baxter, Colin
  Glencoe – Monarch of Glens.
  1. Scotland. Highland Region. Glencoe,
  Description and Travel.
  I. Title II. Crumley, Jim 1947-
  914.118504859

ISBN 0-948661-15-1

Front cover photograph
Buachaille Etive Mór

Back cover photograph
Looking toward Glen Etive from Beinn a' Chrulaiste

Printed in Great Britain by
Frank Peters Printers Ltd., Kendal.

Glencoe
Monarch of Glens

Colin Baxter
&
Jim Crumley

Colin Baxter Photography Ltd., Lanark, Scotland

Glencoe
Monarch of Glens

Acknowledgements

The author wishes to thank Marion Campbell and W. H. Murray
for their kind co-operation.

Chapter One

Monarch of Glens

YOU CAN STAND quite alone in the depths of Glencoe and feel crowded out, jostled by the press of mountains. It is not a place which nourishes a sense of the freedom of wilderness. Rather, it is a place to be ensnared by wilderness.

Some gargantuan creative force set out to caricature the Highlands of Scotland here and overdid the mountains for effect, like a Gerald Scarfe nose. The resulting landscape profile incites reverence or revulsion, and little in between. I stand among those who revere. If you like your mountains well herded and heaped with hints of the Alps, you will learn to love Glencoe, but it will not necessarily be a blissful, untroubled betrothal. And there will always be those to whom even a car journey through the Pass itself is a tense, uneasy affair, to whom the prospect of penetrating Glencoe's folded depths and ridgey heights is a fate too dire and too daft to contemplate.

It is easy to imagine, too, that here is the spawning ground of every Highland cliche, source of an unstoppable river of bad postcard jokes. And surely here was every other Victorian landscape painter's dingy inspiration, surely what Landseer had in mind when he immortalised his red deer stag as *The Monarch of the Glen* (although at its first public showing it was accompanied by a text about Glen Orchy, and a fragment of far Gleann Quoich still called Landseer's Rocks lodges a rival claim).

Here are roadside pipers and Highland cattle which step from the river onto shortbread tins. Here are red deer and golden eagles, sheep and startling rocks, laments and dirges and Fingalian legends, and coach parties and tourists with fold away picnic chairs and climbers and skiers and whisky and waterfalls. Here is the Highland weather at its most contemptuous, rain like prison bars, winds like hacksaw blades, midges with crampons on, clouds encamped on summit, ridge and corrie for a week at a time or flying up from buttress and shoulder on fast shadowy winds.

And here dwells the one dark cloud which even high summer's bluest day can never banish from these haunted mountain walls, which still pours its own

"... a place to be ensnared by wilderness ..."

embittered rains of unforgiveness. Here dwells the spectre of the most overblown, overrated, over-analysed, the most blatantly deified, glorified and lied about event in the whole vast and unenviable repertoire of self-inflicted wounds which characterised centuries of the history of the Highland clans, all their peaces and all their wars . . . the Massacre of Glencoe.

But here too, if you pick your time and place, is solitude, silence, commitment to a majestically cramped mountain realm, a baffling and beautiful maze fashioned from narrow glens and mountain walls and a crazy paving of watersheds. There is much more to Glencoe than the single thoroughfare between Buachaille Etive Mór and Sgòr na Ciche - the Pap of Glencoe - that curving wedge of space between the five unbroken miles of the Aonach Eagach flank and the black buttresses of the Three Sisters. The landmass to the south of the main glen is slashed in every conceivable direction into glens, passes, cul-de-sacs, corries, buttresses, ridges, peaks, and rivers which try logic sorely.

Try this. As you contemplate Buachaille Etive Mór from the road, the river which flows between you and the mountain is not the Coe. It is the Coupall, an unaccomplished runt of a river born in the Lairig Gartain, and it reaches that trough which will become Glencoe on the wrong side of the watershed which spawns the Coe, and so flows east, away from Glencoe. Soon it encounters the Etive (which has many birthplaces of its own around the fringes of Rannoch Moor) at which point it begins to double back on itself, to be met at the other end of the Buachaille by the Allt Gartain, which in turn is also born in the Lairig Gartain, but on the wrong side of that pass's watershed to become the Coupall. The Gartain reaches the Etive at Dalness in one mile. The Coupall, rises yards from the Gartain, reaches Dalness in about ten miles. Such is the nature of this land.

Glencoe is, of all Scotland's wild Highlands, the glen most utterly given over to mountains. The dominance of those mountains is so compulsory that there is almost no scope for other forces either to play on a mind, or, in the days when the glen was most vigorously lived in, to shape a life. Everything which ever happened here, everything Glencoe is famous and infamous for, everything it is revered and reviled for . . . it is all the way it is and it arouses all that it arouses because of the manipulative power of the mountain throng.

W.H. Murray's celebrated mountaineering classic of 1951, *Undiscovered Scotland* argued in a mesmeric final chapter: "when we go among mountains, although they will always produce effects on our personalities, yet whether they are good effects or bad is determined by ourselves. It is our own attitude of mind that determines effects. Always the choice is ours. Like the jungle, mountains are neutral." I have sparred with that single idea for years, ever since Bill Murray's words first stopped my admiration in its tracks. All mountains? *All* neutral? I wonder.

Here in Glencoe more than anywhere else, I have come to question the mountains' neutrality. Here I find again and again the effects of the mountains determining attitudes of mind. The mountains seem to sustain a uniform presence which I can best describe as a kind of unrelenting benevolent intimidation. I have found snatches of something similar in the Cairngorms and the Cuillins, but always you can walk or climb beyond its grasp, find sanctuary in the airier places. Glencoe has no "airier places", not even on the summit of all Argyll, Bidean nam Bian, whose crown is simply a poised pedestal from which other ridges insinuate mind and eye down into labyrinths of mountains. It may be the crown of the maze but it is still locked into the maze. Altitude does not free it. The phenomenon is a thing, I think, of the mountains, not of the mind, hence its all-weather, all-year constancy. Glencoe never eases up.

The effect of that presence does, however, fashion extremes of attitudes of mind. If you thirl to it, accept it for what it is, adopt it willingly as a companion to your every expedition in Glencoe, you accept the landscape on its own terms. You may well find a hand-in-glove relationship with it which will last you a lifetime, and leave you homesick for its aloof embrace. If you baulk at it, Glencoe will always be an uneasy taskmaster. Eventually there may be nothing you can do about it, except perhaps admire it from below and afar.

Introductions to Glencoe are just as uncompromisingly pronounced. Buachaille Etive Mór and Sgòr na Ciche are all the signposts Glencoe has ever needed,

left "... a beautiful maze ... a crazy paving of watersheds ..."
above Sgòr na Ciche, sentinel of the glen

declarations of the landscape's intent however you approach the glen. Pause by the Buachaille going west, and once you have dragged your eyes away from that apotheosis among nature's pyramids, your gaze levels out to the high watershed beyond which the world appears to vanish. What seems like a land bridge has been slung across your path, or a dam holding back a void. It is penetrated by both road and river, however; both then negotiate in the diverse civil engineering techniques of man and nature, the one thousand feet descent through Glencoe to sea level at Loch Leven. After the moor-wide miles of Rannoch, the Coe's mountain walls drop about your mind like shutters.

But if your journey is east along Loch Leven, you may already have wondered why a mountain such as Beinn a' Bheithir is not world famous, so spreadeagled and handsome are its summits and ridges. Then the mouth of Glencoe seems to inhale you and you forget all that has gone before. Going west, you remember Rannoch for its difference. Going east, you forget Beinn a' Bheithir for its sudden irrelevance. Sgòr na Ciche dips one languorous shoulder into the narrowing loch, oak and birch woods swarm warmly over the flank of Meall Mór, and between the two you thread a passage beyond which the memory of Glencoe's mountain neighbours is irretrievable. First, though, there is a small deception to be played out, because it is a woodland realm you have entered. This is Glencoe's western frontier counterpart to the dam of the east, a flimsy screen draped from wall to wall. It is as though Glencoe is coy about showing its true alpine colours until you are ensnared.

Then the screen dissolves and you are swamped by the psychology of mountain walls. First Aonach Dubh, a sheet of rock hung from an unseen summit, scored and fissured, lacerated by the horizontals of tiers and terraces, the verticals of gullies and fault lines, the fabric of glacial and volcanic traumas woven and tailored into the huge and crude sett of a primeval tartan.

Then the Aonach Eagach butts in across the glen, a mountain wall like no other in Scotland, topped at its crux by two miles of the single most exhilarating ridge on the mainland, bettered by common mountaineering consent only in the

Skye Cuillins. Winter mornings do most for the Aonach Eagach, when sunlight hovers halfway down the mountain like an orange snowline. Summer sun floods the glen and greens the walls and plays down the place, but a mid-December sun darts along the rampart, bugles on buttresses, throws pinnacles forward from the mountain mass, darkens and angers the shadows behind, the elemental mountain.

These two walls, the Black Ridge and the Notched Ridge, rebound the focus of your eyes again and again across the glen, urge your thoughts ever deeper into the glen, ever higher into the mountain realms and they conspire to lure and loom the mountains ever closer. Then your eye will alight on a point high above the Aonach Dubh wall where aslant sunshafts halo the glimpsed peak of Bidean nam Bian, a glittering, snow-powed Alp. Yet there is an almost subtle aspect to the manner in which the idea of Glencoe's upper chambers insinuates itself into your mind, that higher and more rarified world beyond the walls, yet within walls of its own. The first hint has been dropped about the scope and scale of the mountain maze.

There is another Glencoe. It is that deep gray place in which a third shutter - of cloud as thick as mountains - clamps down, stripping the glen of its essential form. The walls and the floor of what is left of Glencoe thrum with the rhythms and turbulences of white water. It is that Glencoe which coined the well-worn cliche of the Glen of Weeping. As a translation of the name "Glencoe" it is a nonsense, a fanciful theory with no shred of academic or cultural authenticity, but given the Victorians' disregard for both in their crassly romantic redefining of the Highland landscape, a theory which they gleefully promulgated. There is little argument that Glencoe often appears to weep, even sobs uncontrollably when the rains have drenched down on Bidean and the rest for a fortnight at a time, and there is equally little argument that the intolerable perpetuation of the Massacre fuels the tear ducts of the gullibly misty-eyed. But a sodden mountain is a sodden mountain wherever you encounter one, and the grimmer cheerlessness which Glencoe emits on such days is only a matter of degree, because there are more mountains to weep here than in most places. There is no day when there are not mitigations to behold.

above A coronet of clouds, a monarch of glens
right Loch Achtriochtan awakes to early sunlight

14

The idea that Glencoe is a morbid, melancholy place is simply a misreading of the landscape elements, and an unthinking acceptance of that equally unthinking relic of Victoriana. So many travellers with pen in hand have dashed off travelogue-ish diatribes, and a few of these have won a quite un-merited credibility because of the byline. Writers who should have known better, like Dickens, and writers who never really knew better in the first place, like H.V. Morton, are equally culpable. The following taste of the Dickens outburst is quoted not to further its already celebrated cause, but to show it up for its unquestioning acquiescence to the Glen of Weeping school of thought:

" . . . Glencoe itself is perfectly terrible. The Pass is an awful place . . . there are scores of glens, high up, which form such haunts as you might imagine yourself wandering in, in the very height and madness of a fever . . . The very recollection makes me shudder." H.V. Morton waxed even more hysterical in his book *In Search of Scotland*:

"A man suddenly shot up into the moon might gaze at the cold remote mountains with much the same chilly awe that he looks at the Pass of Glencoe. Here is a landscape without mercy. So far as Glencoe is concerned, the first germ of life has never struggled from the warm slime . . . "

That was from a book which between 1929 and 1935 sold out twenty-one editions, which is a lot of misrepresentation. The kindest thing to be said of Morton's search for Scotland is that he simply did not find it. It is not an unknown technique among travel writers to daub their own thumbprints over landscapes and languages which they have neither the inclination to understand nor the time and energy to learn or question. The true meaning of Glencoe is long lost, and researchers have produced only unconvincing and unconvinced best guesses. One Gaelic speaking native of the glen explained to me that when he was a boy there the local Gaelic name was Gleann Comhann, which is roughly the Glen of the Dogs - roughly, because, as he pointed out, there is no such word as Comhann in any Gaelic dictionary. What there is is the word Cumhann, meaning narrow, and as the one is pronounced - again, roughly - "kon" and the other "koon", is is easy to fashion the name of the Glencoe from either of them. He was, however, neither convinced by Cumhann, an opinion shared by researchers, nor could he expand on the Comhann of his childhood. "As a boy, you never think to question such things. Now, the old people are gone."

So I tried him on another theory, my own as far as I know, but I cannot believe that it hasn't surfaced before now. It is that the word Coe could simply be a cartographer's mistake for Ceo - mist - and that the Glencoe is Gleann a' Cheo, Glen of Mist, in the way that Skye is Eilean a' Cheo, the Misty Isle of probably equally fanciful origins. In much the same way, a mistake led to the Laigh (low-lying ground) of Menteith becoming the Lake of Menteith, or so one more theory runs. My Glencoe native was as unimpressed by Ceo as I thought he would be, and as he is both scholar and tutor of Gaelic and I am neither, it should probably be stricken from the record. Perhaps I should have been a Victorian, and Morton could have come among my descendants brandishing my theory like a torch and crying Eureka while the glen overflowed with weeping theories. All that we do know is that we do not know. The name of Glencoe remains an enigma, and as long as the tourist tea towel trade promotes its Glen of Weeping preferences, there is no serious prospect of facts - especially irritatingly inconclusive facts - from being permitted to cloud the issue.

One thing which Dickens, Morton and the rest share is the fact that the glen left its mark on their sensibilities. Another is that they heaped the scorn of passing acquaintance on a landscape which responds best to an oath of allegiance and long and loyal and diligent service in the fathoming of its regal secrecies. For if ever there was to be a hierarchy of glens, surely this would be its Head of State. Whether King or Queen is immaterial, but a Monarch of Glens, certainly.

Chapter Two
Alleyways for Eagles

I T IS the south side of Glencoe which makes the place what it is, that litany of
mountain shapes and spaces shepherded into their ragged westering flock by the
Herdsmen of Etive . . . Buachaille Etive Mór (the Great Herdsman of Etive,
affectionately known as just The Buachaille), the Lairig Gartain, Buachaille Etive
Beag (the Small Herdsman, affectionately the Wee Buachaille), the Lairig Eilde,
Beinn Fhada, Coire Gabhail, Bidean nam Bian, Stob Coire nan Lochan, the
buttresses of Gear Aonach and Aonach Dubh (which with the fag-end of Beinn
Fhada masquerade as The Three Sisters), An t-Sron, the Fionn Ghleann, Gleann
Leac-na-Muidhe and Meall Mór. It is a bludgeon of a landscape for the unwary
traveller, but it is nothing more than a well-worked facade, the ends of mountains
and the beginnings of passes and corries.

Yet to the most cursory of travellers it is all the Glencoe there is - that and
the Massacre, of course. Certainly, it reeks of the breath of Glencoe, insinuates
definitions into the mind's eye, but every mountain remnant wedged into the
glen's Ice-Age-trampled flank also unfurls southward the walls of other scaled
down Glencoes of its own, a ragged series of mountain thoroughfares and
no-thoroughfares which dodge and collide with yet more mountain walls deeper into
the maze. Glencoe echoes far down all their contours and corridors and contortions.

It is the north side of Glencoe which unmasks the facade and begins to make
sense, if not of the maze, at least of its entrances and exits. To make true sense of
such labyrinthine landscapes you need a nape of dark gold, an orange eye, a
seven-feet wingspan, a hand-in-glove way with the whims of wild winds and a
crushingly calculating way with the ridge-running mountain hare, for such places
are the alleyways of eagles. But a slow two-mile contour along Glencoe's north
flank at about 2000 feet is a reasonable compromise for earthbound mortals.

The altitude matters. In the glen you see only the facade. From the north
wall's summits you are on equal terms with the highest ridges of the maze and
overlook the mysteries. From halfway between, at about 2000 feet, the land across
the glen still climbs to your eye, so the passes are put in their lowly place, but the
summits still dwell eagle-free above you, or flirt in and out of sightlines behind

The masquerading buttresses of the Three Sisters

19

laddering ridges. The landscape is explained, unfolds its scale, but not its mysteries.

From such as Stob Beinn a' Chrulaiste (which thrillingly contemplates the Buachaille), by way of Beinn Bheag, across the Devil's Staircase and as far west as A'Chailleach, every southward glance across the glen penetrates deep into that taut, high-rise mountainscape. Passes open sesame as far as the watershed, and mountain shoulders and ridges spreadeagle obliquely, the whole gangling majesty of it pinned like the flailed banners of a petrified maypole to the centre-piece of Bidean nam Bian. All south Glencoe is rooted to that summit or defers to it.

It is the north side of Glencoe, too, which heightens the dramatic darkness of the Three Sisters by girdling its unbroken wall clear across their northern horizon, so close that from the deepest recess of the glen it seems to cocoon all that remains of the world, an overbearing proximity. Without that north wall, the Sisters would gaze boldly out across Rannoch Moor and the broad valley of the Leven to the Mamores. Dickens and Morton and Glencoe's other famous detractors would have had nothing to get so thoroughly neurotic about, and there would have been no glen-of-weeping nonsense for historians to debunk.

So the north side of Glencoe is a crucial element in the glen's notoriety as well as in defining the rigidity of its landscape. At its eastern end, and about halfway up the wall, it offers those intriguing insights into the more compelling mountain world to the south. The contrast is nowhere more defined than right at the outset of the glen, where Beinn a' Chrulaiste and Buachaille Etive Mór keep stoical watch in the teeth of the unhindered winds and weathers of Rannoch Moor. No two mountains were ever less equally matched. The Buachaille is surely on every Scottish mountaineer's list of their top five mountains anywhere, a superstar among mountains, home to superstars of mountaineering, and a pivotal place in Scottish mountaineering history. Beinn a' Chrulaiste is on no-one's list of anything, save perhaps the most dogged of Corbett collectors, and my own unwritten list of viewpoints from which to watch superstar mountains flaunt their superstardom.

Buachaille Etive Mór's
an anthem among mountains
how the Pyramids might look
if God had made them by the book.

Beinn a' Chrulaiste, its unsung neighbour's
a mountainous slump, but owns
one song, one choral fame
the Buachaille cannot claim:

from here alone unfurls the score
of anthemed Buachaille Etive Mór.

The trick works best in winter. W.H. Murray, revered hereabouts as mountaineer and mountaineering scribe, is one of the more perceptive writers to have been moved by Glencoe. He wrote: "The closer one's approach to beauty, the more pronounced grows that seeming austerity; on hills such true beauty would seem more evident in winter, just as it comes out in the character of men more in times of challenge than in days of ease . . . "

It is that quality of beauty-through-austerity which characterises the winter glen. If you tread that 2000 feet contour west from Beinn a' Chrulaiste as the lowest sun of the year ducks down behind the Buachailles and dips towards the shoulders of Bidean nam Bian, the show of sun and shadow and cloud and summit snow and mountain shapes is a perpetually shifting rearrangement of austere beauties. From Stob Beinn a' Chrulaiste, a tiny plateau overhanging the Glencoe road, a mid-morning-to-mid-afternoon mist seethes softly in from Rannoch like the imperceptibly moving slack water of a high tide. But under the Buachaille it catches in the warp and weft of the Herdsman's plaid and crampons up the mountain in a gray-white swarm. The sun's answer to such an advance is to punch holes in it, once to flood the base of the mountain beneath the mist so that you watch the drama of the Buachaille across the lit footlights of its stage. What was it Dickens said? "Glencoe itself is perfectly terrible." Perhaps he foresaw the following:

I sit in awe of my mountain idyll, marvelling at the Buachaille across the glen because, well, because it's the Buachaille, when a jet creeps soundlessly out of Glen Etive, shimmies west round the Rannoch Wall, flips north at Altnafeadh, until at 600 - or whatever - miles an hour, the sound catches up and bellows from wall to wall of the glen, belches up the Devil's Staircase in (about) two-and-a-half seconds, while I mouth my wrath at its wake. The sound subsides. The fury takes a little longer.

The last two hours have been consumed with thoughtfully stalking and photographing ptarmigan in winter garb, yet the image which will haunt the memory of those hours is of a jet wedged in the thrapple of the glen. But the antidote is already wing-dipping through the Lairig Eilde, whispering across Stob nan Cabar of Buachaille Etive Beag, wheeling east-nor-east to cut a mighty eye level swathe past my outpost. The eagle crosses the jet's flightpath five minutes after it had passed, too near a miss for the comfortable coexistence of eagle and jet. He flings me a side-headed glance in his passing, wings set in what friend and eagle champion Mike Tomkies calls (wryly apt in the circumstances) a "jet glide", a sustained shallow dive which he has measured at speeds above 100 miles per hour. Such prolonged sprinting is often a device to shake off the irksome attentions of querulous peregrine, raven or crow, and as the eagle drops behind my hill I wheel the glasses back in the direction he came from. At first, nothing, but then, fully two minutes later, two ravens beat frantically down his wake, croaking with every other wingbeat, a faintly hysterically falsetto edge to their calls. By the time they too disappear behind the hill they have covered at least four flat-out miles to deliver the most futile of protests. Corvid psychology is one of the least fathomable in nature.

Moments later, the eagle re-emerges almost overhead, flying somewhere around 4000 feet, and there, like the tortoise's doggedly daft pursuit of the hare, are the ravens, puffing up the mountain wind. At this last supreme daftness, the eagle falls on the ravens as they climb, a prospect sufficiently daunting to persuade them into retreating disarray, arcing wildly down the sky like black rocket sparks. The eagle charges on and down, levels out to a new shallow glide. He is back over the Devil's Staircase in (about) two-and-a-half seconds, after which the jet is just a nasty taste in

"... anthemed Buachaille Etive Mór ..."

the mouth. A year later, however, it is the jet, not the eagle, which recalls the hour, and in a landscape such as Glencoe where eagles' airspaces should remain uninfringed by anything more insidious than ravens, that *is* perfectly terrible.

Through all that, the sun and I have westered (the sun has circumnavigated Etive and its Buachailles and I have crossed the Devil's Staircase) at our own languorous pace, and rooted again, polar opposites, with the length of the Lairig Eilde and the width of Glencoe between us - well, most of the length of the Lairig Eilde, for that south-westering pass dips wickedly south right on the watershed confounding many a mist-plaided walker, and from here, its southernmost mile is hidden from sight. That Pass of the Hind swathes in colour, but such an indefinable shade, neither primary nor pastel, that for all its hints of yellow, pink, orange, brown, it is conclusively none of these. It is, too, a curiously flimsy shade, a frail thing to be so compelling in a landscape of such substance, as though Landseer's canvas had been infiltrated by Monet. Such a sun also blackens every rock and runnel and gully and hummock and hollow, and these punctuate the floor and flanks of the pass thick as stubble, rendering the colour-questing all the more fruitless.

But now the sun has reached that fragment of its world's arc which, from my hoodie's eye-view on the snout of A'Chailleach, throws a fan of shadowy beams across the Glencoe mountains, as though a flimsy and askew Venetian blind has been dropped over the landscape.

From a hub somewhere low and deep and unseen in Glen Etive, rods of light tip and bar the world from the summit of Bidean nam Bian to the colour-brimming mouth of the Lairig Gartain. The buttresses of the Three Sisters are blunt shrouds (it is past the season of sunlight for the buttresses, they are Sisters of the shadows until spring now), but the highest crest and the bowsprit of Beinn Fhada smoulder a smoky-gray orange. The summit snows of Stob Coire nan Lochan are lit the most pastel of blues in that most oblique of lights, a startling luminosity about the snows so much more beguiling than the dazzle of direct sunlight; Bidean nam Bian wears a deeper shade of the same hue, for this is one of the few viewpoints in the glen from which Bidean and Stob Coire are aligned one behind the other, although the roller coaster ridge between them is well hidden. Other beams climb all but vertically up the flanks of Stob Coire Sgreamach and Sron na Lairig at the end of the Lairig Eilde, impaling their lancing light on a cloudless shield of whitening skies. Still others finger the depths of the Lairigs, dusting the edges of Buachaille Etive Beag. Then the sun slips behind some unseen impediment in the landscape and the show is done, the fan folded, the sky-fires smoored. Immediately the gloom amid the Sisters is relieved, detail emerges in Coire Gabhail and Coire nan Lochan, not because any more light has been brought to bear, but because eyes have adjusted and, in the absence of the sun's sorcery, consent to the challenges of the shadows. The green "meadow" of Coire Gabhail (the Corrie of Capture, of much cattle-rustling myth and some fact) is suddenly glaringly visible. That visibility intrigues, and I wonder just how few people have wandered here where I stand. It has little enough appeal to today's peak-bagging, ridge-hopping obsessions, and all the good rock-climbing is elsewhere. It is a place only for the unravellers of landscapes. The Glencoe people of old must have known it for an untrodden place too, for there would have been little point in hiding stolen cattle in such as Coire Gabhail if prying eyes were accustomed to wander the one hill flank which peers directly into the sanctuary at eye level.

The Macdonald's cattle-rustling exploits have always been pinch-of-salt stories, but there seems little doubt that it happened to a certain extent. Driving cattle up into Coire Gabhail would have been no meagre feat, however, given the nature of the corrie's bouldery defences. It is just possible, . . . if there were enough opportunities to make cattle rustling a lucrative pastime, that the most difficult parts of the climb could have been built up by the Macdonalds to make them easier for cattle to negotiate. But again, any regular passage of people and cattle in and out of the corrie must have left the most visible of trails up the mountainside, so that you wonder if the true value of Coire Gabhail was not the secrecy of its "Lost Valley" but the fact that it was particularly easy to defend with a handful of guards. Perhaps, perhaps . . . the train of thought trails off as the light begins to fade. Eyes wander away.

As the murk begins to gather darkly in the east, the Glencoe road gives every appearance of a weary highway to another world, the unencapsulated moody sprawl of

left The approach to Coire Gabhail, haunt of cattle rustlers
above "... every airspace is uncompromisingly sculpted ..."

Rannoch Moor, where nothing is defined or shaped or enclosed. That too is part of the mysticism of Glencoe, for immediately you enter in at its portals after Rannoch, it stamps itself on your mind as everything in landscape which Rannoch Moor is not. Retrace the glen westward again; by A'Chailleach, how deeply embedded in the glen and its psychology you have become, how hemmed in and held you are, how remote from Rannoch. The road falls and falls away to that treed shore under Sgòr na Ciche. Loch Achtriochtan lies before the trees, a slab of gray slate.

Suddenly a ragged bird falls fast down the mountainside, flutters, brakes, perches; a soft call grates against the wind suggesting the last wheeze of a terminally ill petrol lawnmower. A solitary fieldfare is working along the mountain flank, the barren miles under the Aonach Eagach newly negotiated, diving desperately down into every gully and nook and cranny, a forlorn quest for berries. Only the gullies hold trees on this side of the glen and these are wind-blasted, spate-tormented, rock-rooted spindles with no vestige of red to their name.

I ponder the bird's dilemma. I know what it may well not know, which is that if it's berries it seeks (and it is - it always is with winter fieldfares) it's eastering when it should be westering, and given that it's eastering, it's on the wrong side of the glen to veer naturally into Glen Etive which leads to kindlier lands for berries and Scandinavian looters and pillagers. If the fieldfare holds this course, the next rowans are probably somewhere around Glen Orchy - a long pech on an empty stomach.

The bird's progress is watched by a resident hoodie which has a cannier way with the airspaces of the glen, and having lingered over a helpful thermal by A'Chailleach, lifts away across the glen to the folded skirts of the Sisters, the flight cut at an ungainly diagonal, led by the primaries of a starboard wing, head scrutinising forward and down.

The hoodie's slanting flight, the eagle's deft dismissal of the ravens, the recalled cleaving whiteness of two whooper swans through an early spring evening . . . all these sharpen the focus of Glencoe's other great elemental distinction - it's airspaces. The nature of this landscape is such that every airspace is uncompromisingly shaped and sculpted from the vee trough of the main glen to the U shapes of the Lairigs, the boomeranging Gleann Leac-na-Muidhe, the high-backed tapering scoops of Coire Gabhail and Coire nan Lochan, the back alley of Gleann Fhaolain, the tight wedge hammered snugly into the Fionn Ghleann. The containing mountains sharpen the edges of the airspaces, heighten and shape their dramatic effect, fashion a raggedly interlocking stage on which birds and cloud and mist and wind and weather perform. They are no less dramatic than the mountains themselves.

If you contour round above the watershed of the Lairig Gartain towards the neighbouring watershed of the Lairig Eilde, and if the cloud level of 3000 feet is lingering 1000 feet above the snowline, there is a point under Stob na Bròige of Buachaille Etive Mór at which you emerge from one of a series of narrow screes to confront the baulking right-angle of Stob Coire Sgreamach and Beinn Fhada. In just such circumstances, I watched the adventures of wind and light and cloud and snow, and startled a roving flock of snow buntings into retreat far round the mountain. Their small flecked cloud adrift above the watershed of the Lairig Eilde reconstituted that right-angle of rock and snow before me as a meeting of two airspaces. The birds drifted from one to the other, but long after they had vanished and the small song of them subsided, I looked into that convulsion of mountain forces and saw only the junction of flightpaths, only the shapes made by the air.

Such are the thoughts which can wing free from A'Chailleach on the north wall of Glencoe in the wake of a cavorting hoodie crow, but no train of thought here dwells free of the mountains for long. Slowly the jagged regime of summitry re-establishes its omni-present control.

The earth cracked open here. Glencoe's birth throes tore open the rock in volcanic grins, now the gullies of headlong burns or foul-weather waterfalls. Miniature woodlands and hanging gardens hide in such places where bell heather and gentians flower on into mild Decembers, untroubled by sheep, and spared the worst wrath of wind and frost. One gully often has a mirror image across the glen - mighty Clachaig for example, has a less illustrious counterpart disfiguring An t-Sron where a single fault line has fractured both mountain walls in one titanic hiccup. Likewise, the gully by A'Chailleach could well have won landscape stardom rather than anonymity were it

above New shadow, old snow, Stob Coire nan Lochan
right "The earth cracked open in volcanic grins"

30

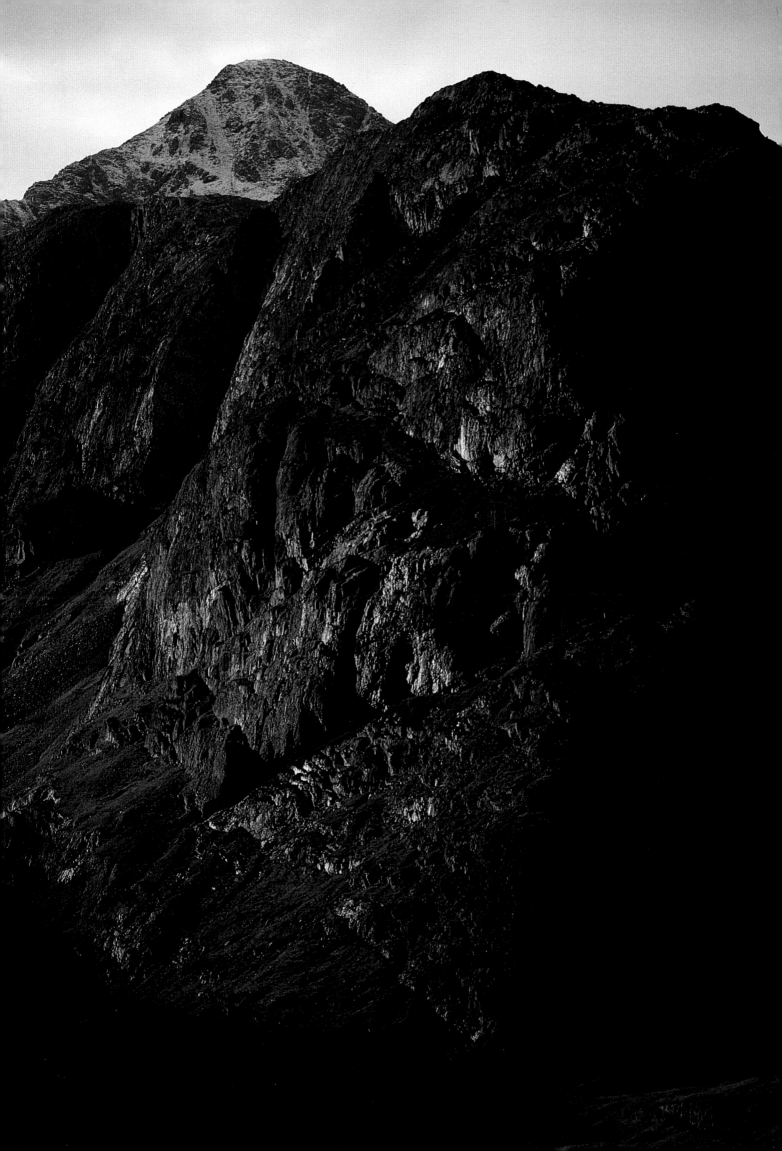

not twinned right across the glen floor in a single gawping trench with one of Glencoe's landscape superstars. Coire Gabhail is not only a stupendous gully, not only a small forest rooted in impossible rock flanks and an awesome tumbledown of boulders, but also, above all that, the most sudden, startling and self-contained flat-bottomed, rock-walled overworld that mountain treasure seekers might dare to dream. Coire Gabhail is the "Lost Valley" of much thoughtless publicity in recent decades. I was once stopped by a passing Cadillac (a more incongruous species in Glencoe than a Campbell wake) and hailed thus:

"Hey buddy, I'm a Macdonald, how do I find the Hidden Glen?"

Despite the fact that it has been crudely serviced by the National Trust for Scotland with three roadside car parks and a wooden staircase and bridge to negotiate the gorge of the Coe (this controversy is explored in detail in Chapter Five), Coire Gabhail never ceases to take me aback. Every new crossing of its great boulder screen still has the air of a sacred threshhold. I have found something similar only twice - in Iona Abbey, and on Dunadd, hill capital of the tribal ancients of Argyll.

What is it about these few high acres and their hemming Alpine skylines which raises a human consciousness above and beyond those demands which all Glencoe makes? For me there are two answers. Firstly, even for Glencoe's mountain maze, Coire Gabhail is an extraordinary gathering of mountains, its walls stepping raggedly and all but vertically on three sides. I have sensed it with the sky a gray canopy at 2000 feet like nothing so much as the open coffin of a giant of unimaginable proportions. Clear-skied it is the ruin of an equally inconceivable abbey. With a glittering snow cornice on Bidean's south-east ridge and the aftermath of a whirling snow-wind on the corrie's flanks it is that same abbey ruin draped in silks, trimmed with lace. In all these garbs, Coire Gabhail is entered as from another, lesser world.

Secondly, Coire Gabhail challenges more forcefully than anywhere else in Glencoe, the notion of the neutrality of the mountains. There is a sense here of the kernel of all Glencoe, a reservoir of that presence which is a constant companion through the mountain maze. Here it is at its most intense, here it is most palpably the work not of minds but of mountains.

I am aware that by writing of such a place in such terms I invite the accusation of exacerbating the destructive pressures of too many trampling feet on the fragile mountain soil, too much gaudy, noisy people-littering of that sacred ambience which I claim for Coire Gabhail. My reasoning is this: I believe there is a duty among those who write about landscape to further its highest ideals, and in so doing to enhance in the reader a sense of respect for that landscape in the belief that he will tread it more thoughtfully as a result. If, as I believe, the best of our landscapes suffer from poor management, then it is the writer's duty, too, to show what it is at risk, and why. It is my considered request for Coire Gabhail that until such time as a wiser counsel prevails in the management of Glencoe that you walk softly and drink deeply when you tread its embrace. The pendulum of public consciousness is swinging back towards landscape, to savour it and serve its best interests. Perhaps when it has swung a little further, a movement will emerge to persuade the National Trust for Scotland to undo its policies at Coire Gabhail, to dismantle bridge and staircase and allow the hill grasses to invade the car parks again; to accord Coire Gabhail once again the protective isolation of the moat with which nature endowed it.

The moon is up over Beinn a' Chrulaiste as I wander back, ballooning across the confusing skies of dusk. The road below is quiet, the Devil's Staircase the thoroughfare only of ghosts. A blackened Indian file of red deer - four hinds - eases down a skyline shoulder, and a flaky shape I cannot identify is spinning slowly down the frosted air. I watch it settle soundlessly on the heather fifty yards away and carefully mark the spot. As I cross the intervening ground, I become aware of an eagle trekking north high over Beinn Bheag. There is no mistaking its stride, its windmill sail wings. By my feet at the spot I had marked lies a sprig of holly, about eight inches long. There is no wind, no tree within half a mile. This is my mysterious spinning shape, that the eagle which dropped it, or so I choose to believe. The human mind can be forgiven for imbuing tokens from above with all manner of significances when it roams alone through the alleyways of eagles. The unflattering rasp of a hoodie drifts on the air across a mile of Glencoe. The voice harps on and on. I think he is laughing at me, but I will carry the eagle's holly home.

Chapter Three

The Valley of the Shadow

H ISTORY HAS ALWAYS seemed a more tangible part of the landscape it strutted when winter stalks its birthplace. The quiet days of early winter, before the big snows and the big migration of climbers and skiers are the best to delve into the glen that was. The glen is pared away to the elemental bone and landscape forces predominate unhindered by the diversions and distractions of people herded into uncivil numbers. These seasonal invasions, and the almost total absence of a native population in Glencoe itself, are the opposite of the way things used to be. For much of history, Glencoe sustained a thriving population, many small farms, anything up to a thousand head of cattle, and a stranger wandering through the glen was a conversation piece which could last a week. The most frequent adjective used of Glencoe in older records is "fertile". Look at the sheep-shorn land and mourn.

Apart from the familiar mountain shapes, you and I would have difficulty recognising the Glencoe of, say, the 15th-17th centuries. There would be many houses, much well-worked land and miles of dykes, especially at the edges of the low ground where spates and rockfalls created all manner of havocs on the cultivated ground. Most astounding, it would be a well-wooded place, there would be only handfuls of sheep, and no through road. The reek of woodsmoke, or peatsmoke, or both would be on the air, and the place would resound to the sights and sounds of a tight community going about the workaday business of living off the land - their own and other people's.

The best of it would have been idyllic. It would have been a handsome place to live and there would have been the distinction of the uniqueness of their mountain realm for the natives to wear like a badge in the company of others from beyond the glen. The worst of it (long winters after bad growing seasons, a meagre booty of undernourished cattle stashed away in Coire Gabhail, a father or a favoured son lost to the eternal bloody bickerings between clans) must have been a misery which few of us could either thole or contemplate. It is an uncanny tribe of ghosts whose company you keep when you ford the river in pursuit of that way of life which was, whose echoes and artefacts still linger in the folds of the Sisters' skirts, or tucked away discreetly into the quiet curve of Gleann Leac-na-Muidhe.

"The quiet days of early winter are the best . . ."

The Alpine nature of Glencoe is at its most psychologically demanding on the low ground. The buttresses frown through winter's sunless months, and the north wall throws unrelenting confinement about the floor of the glen; at times it must have felt like living in a suit of armour.

You fall to wondering as you creep under Gear Aonach how much the landscape contributed to the character of those who lived here when travel beyond the glen was undertaken only in dire necessity. How did such a rarified environment equip and affect them in landscapes beyond, how did they mould their lives within it? The recorded and reputed forays into neighbouring lands over many years suggest that the landscape's biggest contribution to the wellbeing of the people of Glencoe was one of defensive strength. It felt safe to be in the glen, it would be easy to defend, so much so that it almost certainly never occurred to any of the Macdonalds' rivals to attack them directly on their own ground, hence the deception which was necessary to effect the Massacre of 1692. It is safe to speculate that their neighbours regarded the Macdonalds and their exclusive mountain world with some awe. To that extent, the Glencoe landscape worked in their favour, the perfect terrain from which to launch guerrilla raids and to retreat to with the spoils, a secure land in which to raise crops and children.

For all that, there must have been times when the confinement of its physical limitations weighed heavily on the restless spirits of the younger men, especially in dire winters. You can feel the faintest echoes of it walking through the five hours of half light of a drab December morning and afternoon, your sixth successive day lodged in a tent in the glen, when nothing like sunlight has glimmered through the peaks, when seemingly all life has been padlocked by weeks of frosts, and the ice edges slowly out from the shores of Loch Achtriochtan towards the two restlessly feeding whooper swans. On the seventh dark dawn, the swans, too, have retreated, and doleful winter bears down a little heavier. To that extent, the Glencoe landscape was a burden.

The surprise of the buttresses of the Three Sisters at close quarters is how wooded they are. Aonach Dubh rears in uncountable tiers and rock faces, all of which seem to support small growths of birch, rowan, oak and holly. The sheep rarely forage here so the trees survive even on such minimal nourishment. Such trees, and the dense woodlands of the west end of Glencoe, hint at how the low ground must once have looked before the Clearances, before the sheep. It is tempting to think that now that the glen is owned by the National Trust for Scotland, and does not *have* to pay its way as farming units, and now that there is such a growing public awareness of the worth of wild landscape, the climate is perfect to re-establish something of the native woodland that was. It would gladden Highland hearts to see a blaze of autumn oak around Loch Achtriochtan, to watch their green and softening landscape speech advance amid the guttural rockforms of the spring glen.

A ragged wall emerges from the gloom, an old enclosure with huge boulders incorporated - presumably where they lay - into the drystane dyking. The wall follows the line of least resistance to the contours of the land, rather than trying to impose any set shape on them. The corners are neither round nor right-angled, the walls shapeless, without so much as a straight yard. The place recalls the dykers of St Kilda who built with what was to hand, whose enclosures knew no shape as formal as square or circle. This dyke of Glencoe sits far happier in its landscape by virtue of its shapelessness, than, say, its Borders counterpart. It rises and falls and swerves with the land, shaped into shapelessness by the land. It is a work of some ingenuity and much fluidity, but the Glencoe natives of old would have need of dyking skills. All round the base of the buttresses are huge screes and the litter of old rockfalls; these and anything up to a hundred inches of rainfall a year conspired to do their worst on the labours of the dykers. There would be much ingenuity and craftiness built into their efforts to withstand such forces, and much deft repairing where their ingenuity failed.

I followed the dyke down towards the river. A small long-billed bird rose a yard ahead, dull brown with hints of green across its retreating back. It flew directly and silently for twenty yards then took to the bracken and grasses again. I assessed the evidence for a few moments, having diagnosed "snipe" at first glance

then succumbing to instant doubt as it flew off, smaller, thicker-set, straight and silent. It was a jack snipe, something of a speciality of the Coe's lower reaches in winter, a loner, a skulker, a wanderer amid the dust and spoor of the old ways and those who trod them. It is easy, alone and on such a day as this, to know a fellow feeling with a jack snipe in Glencoe.

The bottom end of the old enclosure runs above the river bank, then veers raggedly uphill again towards the buttresses. From its lowest point the traces of another dyke, straighter this time, and no more than knee-high and smothered in turf and moss, leads pointedly to the skeleton of a cottage. Even in roofless decrepitude its stonework bears the brushstrokes of an accomplished art, although one associated more with the Western Isles than Argyll. Robert J. Naismith writes in his masterly book, *Buildings of the Scottish Countryside:*

"In the older buildings in Lewis . . . the walls . . . stand out from the thatched roofs which rest near the inner face. The drystone walls, with round corners to deflect the wind, have large central cavities filled with turf or similar material. The top of the walls are bedded with thick turf. This cavity wall insulation far out-performed the modern equivalent. The builders also knew that the point where the eaves meet the outside wall is the most vulnerable part of a structure in a gale. So they wisely set back the thatched roofs for protection. The surrounding ledge at roof level served as a platform for repairs and rethatching. Inside on a wild night the crofters did not need to have fear for the furious winter rages. They neither felt the wind nor heard it." Here in Glencoe is a house which bears many of those hallmarks, the only substantial ruin to bear witness to the community which once populated the glen. "Now and then we passed a hut or two," wrote Dickens, "with neither window nor chimney and the smoke of the peat fire rolling out at the door," as sniffily dismissive of the builders' genius and sense of place as he was horrified by the landscape.

Close by stands a small, square-ish outbuilding, its site determined by the presence of two large boulders close together, which with a little infilling have become a gable end. The builders' job then became three walls, not four. Simple.

In the mountain maze – towards Etive from the Lairig Gartain

Simple, if that is, you have the instincts and the skills to mould the broken fragments of a collapsed mountainside to your bidding.

What distinguishes these buildings, and every assembly of stones in Glencoe from screes to shingles to riverbeds to old bridges on the Military Road and new footpaths up to Coire Gabhail, is the range of colours. That cottage gable, caught in the flush of a spring evening or the glistening aftermath of a winter deluge, registers a deep pink, lilac, purple, every shade of gray and brown, occasional greens and a startlingly incongruous sky blue. The lintel, a long and evenly shaped piece of what looks like slate, lies before the cottage like a doormat. Whose home? How old? How many generations bowed beneath that lintel? It is thought there was a community of Macdonald bards here, and certainly the site would be a happier choice for aesthetics than for the practicalities of agriculture. It stands hard by the river, and would have every shade of speech in the river's vocabulary for a constant companion. Above, the glen narrows and bends into the pass. The prying eyes of Am Bodach, the Old Man, peer down from the Aonach Eagach ridge. Below, the glen fans past the loch, curves and dips through the trees to the unseen shore of Loch Leven. Behind, all is the sombre shadow of the winter buttresses of the Sisters. Add the old trees, remove the road, punctuate the lower ground with other fires and folk and buildings and beasts. It would have been a good place to live in its heyday, a place fit for the recording of the deeds of those who lived deep in the Valley of the Shadow.

Walking down beneath the Three Sisters is one of the more thoughtful adventures of Glencoe, the antithesis in its landscape of the Aonach Eagach ridge - there is nothing lower and firmer underfoot, nothing darker, nothing wider than this corner of the glen. Other fragments of that older order of Glencoe settlement surface here and there, among them a stone-bottomed path which at one point nudges you up a gentle ramp to a short and well-founded causeway skirting one of the boggier acres of Loch Achtriochtan's flood plain. Here too, you wonder about the purpose of such a path. Like the Military Road on the far side of the glen, it has a desolate air about its winding because it no longer has a destination. Whose hands laboured at these foundation stones, whose eye pronounced the work well fashioned, how many centuries of whose feet threaded the path's course between farms, or enclosures - or what? Was this the oldest main road through the glen? (Even the Military Road is an upstart newcomer of the 1780s, and even then it was a daring course to bludgeon straight through the glen. Thirty-five years earlier, Government troops had slung a road of sorts up the Devil's Staircase to Kinlochleven, giving the glen a wide berth, but that was before Culloden, the unimaginable. With the road through the glen came irrevocable change - industry, sheep, clearance; never was Glencoe so ruthlessly by-passed than the day they opened the road which pierced its hearts.) So this path I threaded through the December chill may well have been the last road which the Glencoe people built for themselves to service their own needs. It is idle speculation perhaps, yet to touch and tread old and well-worked stone is to run out the most tangible thread of communication through the stored centuries of Glencoe's past. It is not a worthless ritual if it fosters a respect and throws a lingering thought after those who held and hefted and laid stone on stone, those who trod the path ushering beasts or bearing burdens of crops or bracken for thatching, those who went in and out at the lintel which now grows its own shroud of moss and lichen. Shut the modern road from your mind, shrug your shoulders at the numbing intrusion of low flying jets which plague today's glen, hold an old, cold stone, and curse the vile legacy of the Clearances which drained the lifeblood from the Glencoes of this country and left the land an anaemic shell.

The river dissipates its energies just above the loch through a hundred-yards-wide sprawl of bouldery shingle, a deceptively demure water after a long dry autumn and weeks of winter frost. A few drenching days will change all that: here-today-gone-tomorrow waterfalls will whitewash every gully on both sides of the glen, and every gully on both sides of every side-glen, pass, corrie, ridge and every undefinable inbetween bit of rock from here to the Wee Buachaille. On the wettest of all such days I have ever seen, Colin Baxter and I wandered up into the Lost Valley to watch and photograph the watery madness. The floor of Coire Gabhail, where the burn normally runs respectfully underground, was like a flood plain. We watched two climbers reach the corrie headwall then turn back. As they passed us, they paused to explain in rich Glasgow humour:

"We thought we'd come down to play in the shallow end for a while."

The rain hammered sideways through every aperture in the Glencoe maze, feeding the new waterfalls then wrenching them apart in mid-fall, hammering the cascade to shreds of water which ultimately teemed up with a hundred other waterfalls, an awesome perpetual motion. One waterfall capered far out over a long diagonal ledge on the rockface, but the ledge was already host to its own separate waterfall, a fall within a fall.

All that white rage foregathers in the Coe. The Meeting of the Three Waters seethed like a landscape in revolt, but the gorge of the Coe is accustomed to such things and conducted the madness with ruthless efficiency into the unflappable calm of Achtriochtan. The loch's embrace simply spread and spread until the thing was done.

For now, though, on this sixth day of hard winter gloom, the loch is shrivelled and icing. The preened and discarded feathers of the two whoopers, curved and upturned, lie ensnared in that grasp. How often, in the courtship high jinks of the neighbourhood hoodies will a passing black eye alight on that flimsy whiteness in its ice trap? A day will dawn in later winter, the black wings will stall above the path, the hoodie's black feet will tramp down that avenue of ghosts to the leaf litter of the shore and prise from the highest watermark debris of the loch a small clutch of swan feathers. Blackface wool and swan feathers - there is no better lining for a raucous nursery of infant hoodies. That's how it happened last spring, and doubtless a wheen of springs down the years. Then, when one of the unfledged hoodies fluttered uselessly out of the nest to its death, and a fox made a meagre snack of it, didn't the small bird-gleaners - the robin, the dunnock and the rest, snatch opportunist mouthfuls of discarded hoodie down for their own later nests? Nature provides strangely in such a landscape, and none of its gifts are refused.

No deliberations over the harshness of the fates of man and nature in Glencoe can stave off the shadow of the Massacre for long. Whatever the truths of that outrage - and it has built up impenetrable cornices of myth over the last 300 years -

"...here-today-gone-tomorrow waterfalls whitewash every gully..."

it has, uniquely among the tawdry episodes which litter the story of the Scottish clans, sustained a power to offend far beyond the significance of what actually happened. The historical events which gave rise to the Massacre are well enough documented without regurgitating them here, but what intrigues me, and what should intrigue this book as an exploration of the Glencoe landscape, is the effect that the landscape had on events, and has had in perpetuating a corrupted memorial of these events.

First, because of the nature of the conflict, I proclaim my neutrality, other than the remotest possibility that my name derives from Crum which was a sept of the Macdonalds of Benderloch, and these doubtless had more than a nodding acquaintance with the Glencoe Macdonalds. Another line of unsubstantiated research by a deceased great uncle suggested seventeenth century cattle rustlers from the south of Ireland. The two need not be mutually exclusive, but the one is as likely or as unlikely as the other. If that hints at a Macdonald-ish pedigree, the emphasis is on the 'ish'. I certainly hold no brief for the notion that cattle rustlers of the world should stick together.

So there was a Massacre of Glencoe, initiated not by Campbells but by King William, and in particular by his Secretary of State the Earl of Stair, who as history has thoroughly documented, was more than a little gratified at the failure of MacIain, chief of the Glencoe Macdonalds, to comply with a bureaucratic deadline, the swearing of fealty to the King by the first of January 1692. MacIain, it should be said, was satisfied that he had complied. An excuse was needed to make an example of one clan to bring all clansmen to heel. MacIain provided it, and Stair was delighted. The troops which came into the glen to carry out the Massacre enjoyed the hospitality of the Macdonalds for two weeks before falling on their hosts at 5a.m. on February 13th. Their commanding officer *happened* to be a Campbell - Campbell of Glenlyon, no great friend of MacIain, although by all accounts they had established a convivial relationship by the time the black day dawned . . . just one of many unexplained inconsistencies in the reporting of the events. Perhaps ten others of a force of 130 men bore the name of Campbell, so it was hardly a Campbell plot.

Campbell of Glenlyon, then, was a soldier, with a soldier's job of work to do - in Stair's words, to "root out that damnable sect". He had forfeited his lands and was bankrupt, and by soldiering he made his living. The botched Massacre suggests he was either an incompetent soldier, or he was sufficiently appalled by the nature of his orders to ensure that the damnable sect was not rooted out. In that at least, he succeeded.

He was to "putt all to the sword under seventy", perhaps 350 people, but again, estimates vary wildly. For whatever reason, somewhere between thirty and forty actually died, including MacIain, although his sons lived despite the fact that Stair's orders specifically demanded their deaths. The rest escaped, though others died in vile weather on Rannoch Moor and few neighbouring clans would hide them for fear of the King's wrath descending on them - or Stair's at least. It *was* a hideous episode, it was sneakily done, Glenlyon is not blameless, and it infringed the code of Highland hospitality. For these reasons, the Massacre earned a measure of notoriety, and certainly it outraged London at the time and infuriated other clan chieftains. As a piece of Government propaganda it was disastrous, but what Government before and since, up to and including the present one, has not seen its most cunning stratagems backfire, and doing down one political cause or another in the process?

But the verdict of posterity, to condemn Campbells the world over at best to a music hall joke, at worst to something much more sinister, is hardly the verdict of an honourable sense of justice.

Nor has it been the subject of the most zealous reporting. It cannot be agreed how many died, because it is not known. It cannot be agreed where MacIain died, whether in his principal house in the main glen, or another house in Gleann Leac-na-Muidhe, because it is not known. It cannot be agreed whether the escape was by way of Rannoch, or Leac-na-Muidhe, or Etive, or Coire Gabhail or all of these, nor how many died in the flight (or how few - who would know these wilderness lands better, even in deepest winter, than those who now took to them to save their lives?). Yet the myth-makers have so adopted the episode that it is claimed as fact that MacIain and Glenlyon had played cards on the night of the Massacre, and

"...the very nature of Glencoe, the very arrangement of mountains
...turning eyes and minds forever inwards..."

Glenlyon had accepted an invitation to dinner the following night! It is claimed as fact that a Campbell piper tried to warn the Macdonalds by playing "Women of this glen, take warning" - the very title of the tune is not disputed! And a soldier was overheard - the very words are agreed! - muttering (presumably in a stage whisper) to a stone thus: "Gray stone, if I were you, I would be shifting from here, for great things will happen tonight." And still suspicions were not sufficiently aroused to take defensive measures!

And still the myth persists that this was the direst of all Highland bloodsheds. Yet fifty years earlier, the Macdonalds killed thirty-six Campbells - yes, Glenlyon Campbells - during a wedding, and bad feeling and much bloodshed had been the norm between the clans for two hundred years. Two hundred Macdonalds died in a cave on Eigg at the hands of the Macleods, and who knows how many died when the Macdonalds sought revenge at Trumpan Church on Skye in 1578 by barring the door and setting fire to the church during a service. American poet Richard Hugo wrote of

> . . . the Macdonalds gloating downwind,
> the Macleods in mid-hymn burning.
> Their screams ran away
> to silence in the west roar of air . . .

No, there have been bloodier, nastier deeds than Glencoe, and there have been many viler tribes than the Campbells, yet still the myth persists. The quest for logic and calm appraisal was not assisted, then, by hysterical or over colourful reporting, all of it, naturally enough, slanted towards the victims. Even the normally painstaking Seton Gordon wrote of the pass at the head of Leac-na-Muidhe (where Macdonalds are supposed to have fled) that it is "so formidable that even the deer seldom cross in winter." As an assessment of that corner of the Glencoe landscape, it is nonsense, but all manner of writers have been swept from the path of objectivity.

The most thoughtful, sensitive, and tellingly written assessment of the Massacre is curiously the work of a Campbell. Marion Campbell's exquisite book *Argyll, The Enduring Heartland* argues:

"Let those who sat in judgement at Nuremberg judge this crime also; it is not for armchair historians or liberal-minded twentieth century journalists to decide." Then:

"Nothing can wipe out the bloodstains on the rocks, no thaw will melt the dead-chill of Glencoe. Each generation faces it again, the atrocity itself and the propaganda made of it; but let us have an end now, in this generation. Surely we who have lived through Lidice and My Lai can find some bitter pity for the heirs of Cain."

Yet still the myth persists. The sign in the Clachaig Hotel in Glencoe which reads "No hawkers or Campbells" is a joke, and is readily explained away as such in the hotel. Yet more than one visitor in recent years bearing the name of Campbell has asked if it means what it says. One young couple from Australia were warmly reassured, then explained that they had only asked because they had been turned away from a guest house elsewhere in Argyll when the landlady learned they were Campbells.

Then there is the song, a modern anti-Campbell diatribe which quickly found its way into many repertoires for its singable chorus:

> Cruel is the snow which sweeps Glencoe
> and covers the grave o Donald
> and cruel was the foe that raped Glencoe
> and murdered the house of Macdonald

There is a line about "Those Campbells had orders King William had signed, put all to the sword, these words underlined" (as a historical footnote, the words were not underlined, but why spoil a good rhyme?) then in the third verse, there is this:

> They came in the night when our men were asleep
> This band of Argylls through snow soft and deep
> Like murdering foxes amid helpless sheep
> They butchered the house of Macdonald.

left Meall Mór confronts the westering River Coe
above A hill burn cuts a corkscrew of scree down the glen

At the end of the day, it is only a modern folksong, rather a good one, and the fact that it wallows a touch in regurgitated and erroneous sentiment only confirms that it has an excellent pedigree in the Scottish folk music repertoire. And it hardly complies with Marion Campbell's thoughtful plea. Helpless sheep! The Macdonalds of Glencoe! Hardly!

The only fox in the saga was MacIain, known far and wide as "The Old Fox", and doubtless he had done his share of murdering. The point is not to belittle the song or MacIain, but to show how well the truth has covered its tracks.

I am not alone in having tried to put flesh on the bones of known events, and I am no historian. From what I have read, however, nothing makes sense other than the fact that what happened happened where it did. I have written in *West Highland Landscape*, an earlier collaboration with Colin Baxter, that "I believe that the Glencoe landscape is a brooding preservative, a conducive arena for the conjuring of old bloodsheds. If it had all happened on bright, wind-rinsed Ardnamurchan, it would be but a footnote to history, and not a claim to infamy."

To Ardnamurchan, I might have added Eigg or Skye or Glenlyon. It is the very nature of Glencoe, the very arrangement of mountains, the way they block every sightline turning eyes and minds forever inward, which colours and heightens perceptions of events within these mountain walls. That and the weather they are apt to lure into their teeming midst. You cut no ice with academics or historians with such a theory, but I am convinced by many hours and miles over many years that such a landscape crammed with mountains, sculpted and scooped with small airspaces, floored with the narrowest of confinements, has the power to enshrine those destinies it has shaped.

The Massacre - once the decision was taken that there was to be one - had to be done the way it was done because the Glencoe landscape precluded "formal" invasion. The executioners had to be insinuated into the midst of their victims. If you still want to apportion blame, as much lies with the landscape itself as with any human failing. If you still want to niggle away at reality by perpetuating myth, your greatest ally is the landscape. Every new generation which sets eyes on the glen then encounters the myth and swallows it whole. Eyes and minds and landscape confirm it. It is because of the mountains that the myth persists.

Eigg is an ocean jewel. Trumpan is a rickle of stones on the brim of the Minch. Glen Lyon's mountains stand respectfully back. All their beauties have washed away the bloodstains long since. Their kind of beauties are not Glencoe's.

The Massacre apart, Gleann Leac-na-Muidhe is an unsung footnote to Glencoe, a passing guidebook reference, an "on your left" blur to the coachbound visitor. Yet it is a pale and sunny imitation of the glen itself. It is a long curve with an unbreached flank and a broken flank (one buttress instead of three), and the same encroaching presence about its mountains. The twist is in the tail where is swerves and climbs steeply west up to that beallach which Seton Gordon found so fearsome. It is rather less fearsome than the modern bulldozed road which carves through the glen's lower reaches as far as its two houses and farm buildings. Why is modern living so messy? Think of the Military Road, the old causeway path, the ruined cottage, the dykes, and then mourn the passing of such stonesmiths, or at least the corner-cutting cost-cutting attitudes which deny them scope.

The river, though, is a gem, its gorge a secretive place of many musics, falls, slides, rapids, gurgles, glides. Trees thrive in its sheepless walls. One small island created by the river briefly bisecting is a fruitful revelation of how the old glen would have fared in those long-dead days when it was a true and untrampled wilderness. A dense crop of trees springs from a luxuriant undergrowth - birch, rowan, holly, oak, pine, willow, aspen, a startling gathering.

Leac-na-Muidhe's name is offered without embellishment as "the slab of the churns", a convolution which has surely lost something in time or translation or both. Perhaps there really was a milk-churning complex here noteworthy enough to christen the place, and the 'slab' long buried under moss or turf or bracken. Or perhaps an explanation of sorts lies deep in the glen's most notable feature, that enchanted little gorge. Among the river's most eloquent carvings within the rock walls is a lopsided bowl, perhaps eight feet deep and six across, in the bottom of which have lodged four large boulders. The action of a spate sets the boulders aswirl

New snow and old amid "that litany of shapes and spaces"
on the south side of Glencoe

54

in their natural bowl at the foot of its mighty rock slab, and there is the raw material at least for a Glen of the Slab of the Churns. Besides, the river is just Allt na Muidhe, just "the river of the churns" which suggests that the churns, whatever they were, were "of the river". The guessing game, once you have acquired the habit, is an irresistible element of any tramp through any long deserted glen. Put yourself in the place of the old natives; a cartographer knocks on your door and asks for the name of the glen. It hasn't got one so you answer on the spur of the moment. I'd go for something like "the Glen of the island of the sheep-free trees". It's as good as the Glen of the slab of the churns.

An October sun does not free the frosts in the floor of the glen until well past noon, by which time an eagle has drifted high above Creag Bhan. There is the only eye which can unravel the maze at a glance, the true chieftain of these lands, the one unbroken lineage which holds sway over all the folded wildnesses of Glencoe, the one fathomable history.

I sit deep in the glen, just above the river where it begins to swing south, pausing as I paused by A'Chailleach to assemble some semblance of order in my mind from the chaotic piles and spillages of the rock in the landscape. Mountain shapes now dart down at you and fire across your bows at every compass point like sheets of arrows. The shapes are mostly dark but late autumn's sun slides obliquely across many a flank, daubing the rock ribs and crests with all the shades of flame you can imagine, like outcrops of golden quartz.

Now that I taste the full savour of Gleann Leac-na-Muidhe, I sense more powerfully than anywhere in the main glen the jaws of a mountain snare. Even in the West Highlands, this is a rarified place. To live here was a rarified mountain existence. Even in the heyday of a resident population, when strenuous walking and riding would be part of everyday life, Gleann Leac-na-Muidhe must have had a feeling of entering a blind alley. Perhaps even the Glencoe folk looked askance at their kin who lived up the alley. The beallach to the west is there, of course, but mostly, you don't see it. Instead, the Aonach Eagach veils the north, the combined might of Bidean and Aonach Dubh a' Chlinne overwhelm the east, Creag Bhan to the west and Sgòr na h-Ulaidh to the south hem darkly in, for all the sun's surprising warmth down by the river. Behind, Meall Mór sits in the mouth of the glen like a stopper.

Creag Bhan is steep enough (it is the principle criterion here abouts) to be beautifully wooded, mostly birch, which grows up to at least the 1800 feet contour. In the damp sunless places on that mountain are sprawling masses of alpine lady's mantle and yellow saxifrage. Glencoe is briefly lush here.

Evidence of the old community of Leac-na-Muidhe is all but gone, a few lines of buried dykes, barely discernible squares of stones. I am struck again by two thoughts, both of which echo feelings in Glencoe. The first - how like the Alps the place can feel. The second - oh to have seen the place alive, lived and loved in, to have eavesdropped on conversation and ceilidh, and to have heard such pipe music as we have long since forgotten how to produce. Seton Gordon recorded in 1935 that "the present occupant of the land, while lifting potatoes some years ago, came upon an old pipe chanter here. The chanter may have belonged to MacIain's piper . . . and it is not long since MacIain's hearthstone was still visible . . ."

That chanter, that stone, have taken truths with them into their oblivion which we will never know.

I pause again on the watershed. It is a short but transforming climb. Suddenly there are worlds beyond.

Sgòr na Ciche is framed by the ponderous skyline bulk of Ben Nevis like heavy gray curtains framing a fragile windowsill ornament. The Mamores loll away west, brilliantly lit, rekindling other hill memories of other years. I have a soft spot for the long ridgey days of those mountains, but from here they are simply snow-scrolled glimpses of another land far beyond Glencoe's confinement. West, the land eases down through plantation forests which lie like dull matting across miles of hill. That way lies Loch Etive and Lorn, an altogether meeker kingdom of subtler charms. I turn back for Sgòr na h-Ulaidh, a place hoisted high by diving ridges and watersheds, back into the snare and the maze of Glencoe.

Chapter Four
On the Silver Wrinkles

THE UPPER ECHELONS of Glencoe, the rock faces, ridges and summits, are magnetic places. They are compulsive lures for those mountaineers whose instincts inhabit the hierarchy and the hall of fame of Scotland's mountains. You do not just climb here, you tread the footsteps and grasp the handholds of the founding fathers of Scottish mountaineering, the spoor of an impeccable pedigree. The pioneers - Collie, Naismith, and Raeburn among them - and their disciples and descendants all returned again and again to Glencoe and its addictions, infusing their landscape love affair with the adrenalin of one more challenge and one more.

Although they all climbed elsewhere, for many of them Glencoe was their be-all-and-end-all. The lived-in glen may have declined to a forlorn kingdom of ghosts and echoes, but by the 1890s the climbed-in glen emerged to don the mantle of the Macdonalds' old vigour.

W.H. Murray wrote in *Undiscovered Scotland*:

"The glen below us lay deep in the gray shadow of frost and a gray skin of ice covered Loch Achtriochtan. That men should choose to inhabit such frozen furrows of the earth's crust seemed mad and unnatural. But to balance on the silver wrinkles - ah that was work for wise and enlightened men!"

Murray's silver wrinkles were the wiles and whorls and warts of the Aonach Eagach at night in winter on good snow and under a full moon. He had awaited such a night for seven years, and the gods smiled on his discernment by throwing in a night-long show of the aurora borealis. Murray and his companion parked under Am Bodach, after which "a double traverse was essential for we planned to be eastward bound at dawn." So they simply did the Aonach Eagach both ways in one night.

Murray is the bard of all Scotland's great mountaineering figures, a fluid and elegant writer who was capable not just of enthralling narrative accounts of his climbs like the first ascent of Clachaig Gully, but could also elevate the mountain experience into something altogether richer than the physical climb. He dared to write of the spiritual and philosophical aspects of mountaineering and brought a rare eloquence to its literature. His best books have never been bettered by anyone in fifty years. He wrote of that night on the Aonach Eagach:

"The upper echelons of Glencoe are magnetic places . . ."

"From this part of the ridge we were better able to see Bidean, to see it as a whole mountain - shaped by deep corries, thrusting its strong ridges outward to eight sparkling peaks, down-curving to lesser tops, emerging from the lowly blackness of Glencoe to a crescendo of light at the summit. That was the Bidean nam Bian of our physical world, by its mere presence there calling our hearts to the world inhabited by beauty."

You win such sights and insights by going again and again, by bringing an intimate relationship with the landscape to bear on a scheme which devises the perfect conditions for the perfect expedition, then by turning down seven years - or however long it takes - of imperfect opportunity to achieve the ultimate. There is only profit to be won by gaining that unique respect for the mountain world which is born of familiarity. Even the nomadic Munro-bagger whose addictive quest is for a spurious list full of ticked-off points on the map, must, if he takes pause for thought anywhere, take it here. If Glencoe cannot persuade him of the value of poring and lingering over these mountains again and again through a climbing lifetime, then I pity him for his soullessness.

We are asked to believe that this mountaineering madness of ours began in the summer of 1868 when a Glencoe shepherd called Marquis climbed up to Ossian's Cave on Aonach Dubh by the route now known as Ossian's Ladder, and tied a handkerchief to a tree as proof that he had done it, rather like the Chinese flag which Dougal Haston found on the summit of Everest in 1975, thus substantiating the Chinese claim which many western climbers had doubted. Marquis became the first recorded rock climber in Glencoe, his ascent the first recorded first ascent, which is a pity, because it is hardly an auspicious classic with which to launch a new era of human endeavour. If there is such a thing as a slum in nature, then Ossian's Cave is its prototype. Ken Crocket's *Rock and Ice Climbs* guide to Glencoe records that it was said of this route: "in descent, the last man should not be married", and there are subsequent warnings of its "herbivorous horrors", (it is an unco jungly place) and that, "the ascent cannot be recommended: there have been several bad accidents involving inexperienced parties and loose rocks …"

I endorse all of that, recalling with no great affection or pride a youthful escapade whose details are best left unexplored. Its lessons are deeply etched in the minds of the offenders of which I was one, and even a passing upward glance at that wretched yawning

"Bidean nam Bian … calling our hearts to the world inhabited by beauty …"

piece of rock is enough to reopen old wounds, or at least re-inflict old bruises. We live and learn, the lucky ones. Older and wiser, I hope, I wouldn't touch it now with a bargepole, two top ropes and an escalator.

My mind prefers to dwell on the golden days amid the silver wrinkles. There was, for example, that Tuesday in February ten years ago. There was a good forecast, an early start, a solo amble up through the Lairig Eilde's morning mists, red deer poised gleaming and anxious in the sun, clarity and crampons on the Beinn Fhada ridge, a touch of axemanship on that funny little bit by Stob Coire Sgreamach where the snow had iced up, and a still and sunny hands-in-pockets dawdle up the ridge of Bidean nam Bian to a silent summit. I made that day last for eons. From the Fhada ridge I watched a raven fly the entire length of the Lairig. No yard of the floor of the pass was visible for the mist lay in its trough like a fluffed up pillow. As the bird neared the watershed and entered the sunlight it became a glistening piece of jet, and a new shadow lagged a few yards behind, slipping over the bouldery flank of my mountain. Bird and shadow met on a rock of Stob Dubh, and the bird's call was the only sound in the world.

Ptarmigan panicked before me on the ridge and spun out over Coire Gabhail, a ragged scatter-gun fusillade of birds. I watched them pitch on snowy screes and disappear in the instant, a favourite flourish of all nature's trickery of which I never tire. I found them again with the glasses, bird clowns, sprinting in tandems, standing like white puffins. You cannot be downhearted for long when you keep the company of ptarmigan.

I climbed on perfect snow in perfect weather on a perfect mountain. There was a well-worn groove of weekend bootsteps all the way up the ridge where fat blue cornices licked out at the mountain air. All the way up, and with nowhere to go but the summit, the track of a mountain hare paralleled the spoor of the human convoy, blithely contemptuous of the cornice edge, so that I began to wonder if a hare had ever gone through a cornice, and become one of Glencoe's more bizarre victims. What kind of mission was this for a mountain hare that took it over the summit of Bidean, at 3766 feet, then on down the other side, two miles of ridge running with no food, no shelter in these conditions, and as brilliantly spotlit a moving target for the neighbourhood eagles as any winter-white hare ever offered?

I had the mountain to myself. I sat like a king in State on the summit for hours, an attitude which the mountain itself seemed to reflect, a king in State among mountains. Each time I was inclined to stir and be up and doing, some facet of the mountain, or the mountain world beyond, or skylined Mull, or a new mountain thought would emerge in a new light and compel me to sit on and study its possibilities. It is a curiosity of the Glencoe landscape that few of the big mountains offer riveting panoramas. Even Bidean - and there is nothing higher in all Argyll - is surrounded by such a rough-and-tumble of mountain slices with glens and passes and watersheds spilling out in every direction that the eye roams restlessly and alights on nothing - or at least nothing that is as compelling as Bidean itself. Bidean from its own summit with the snow wreaths about its sprawled limbs and the fall and rise to Stob Coire nan Lochan, finally reveals its own lynchpin importance to the whole Glencoe landscape. On such a day as this, Bidean is wearing more snow than anything else in sight (the Ben is characteristically cloud-shroudedly morose, revealing nothing), and that too burnishes the mountain's distinguished aura, a decorated general amid rank-and-file troopers.

It was in that mood of sublime absorption in the mountain that I began to think about the Coe of old, about Marquis the mountaineering shepherd, about unsung generations of Glencoe mountaineers who lived before the word was invented. Perhaps they climbed to kill deer, perhaps to retrieve livestock, perhaps - who knows - for the sport or the view or any of the other myriad joys of being on the mountain. The fact that no climbs are recorded before 1868 does not mean that no-one climbed before then. It is often argued - with some justification - that the least adventurous people in wild landscapes are the natives. There are many examples of Highlanders and islanders who lack utterly any enthusiasm for exploring their surroundings which outsiders find so irresistible. I remember a conversation with a Shetlander long domiciled on the mainland, in which I enthused about Yell and Foula. "I was never there," she said. "We were in the town."

The same philosophy might assume that the Glencoe people were the least enthusiastic of mountaineers, yet until the Clearances, a working knowlege of the landscape was part of the survival equipment of the natives. They were familiar enough with Coire Gabhail and probably Coire nan Lochan as both a hideaway for cattle and

left "...a new mountain thought would emerge in a new light..."
above **Aonach Eagach from Buachaille Etive Beag**

65

fugitives from the Massacre. They would surely know other sanctuaries and strategic features of the landscape. They would be familiar with the passes, the high summer grasses for pasture, and could probably distinguish between safe rock and unsafe, good snow and treacherous in much the same way as the eskimos can, because their lives might often depend on such knowledge.

Marquis's single recorded exploit shows too that he at least was happy to climb for fun - or for a wager, or to impress a girl, whatever. It is unthinkable that that was all he climbed, or that he was the only one, or that for as long as the glen was home to the vigour of youth there were not eager voices echoing across the ridges and the summit, and possibly the crags and buttresses and gullies as well.

Oh to convene a meeting of ghosts on this summit on this day as the sun dipped down the winter afternoon, of say, Marquis, Collie, Raeburn, Naismith, perhaps a 16th century Macdonald, perhaps the mortal flesh and blood of W. H. Murray to record the minutes with due reverence (for he alone could do justice to the task of immortalising such a gathering) and in the hope that he might garnish it with the kind of tailpiece he would use to such stirring effect in episodes like his conquest of Clachaig Gully:

". . . the mountains of Ardgour rose in sharp outline, yet without substantiality. One looked not *at* them, but into them, as through the mouths of caverns filled with purple haze, and still one looked beyond . . . They delighted not by crude colour, breath-taking as that can be, but with atmospheric subtlety and noble shape. These were the mountains of true vision, not of this world, causing one to mourn his lost splendour during this life of exile, yet rejoicing him with promise of a return. But there is no way of explaining them . . ."

My gathering of ghosts, and especially the Macdonald and Marquis, would be worth hearing on the statement in Crocket's guide that "one very interesting point is the continuing emphasis on aid reduction and, more important, routes without aid." You might have trouble explaining the meaning of "aid" to a climber of 1868 or 1568.

So I immersed in the fantasy of such a gathering, devising dialogues, bones of contention, common bonds, philosophies, how to explain the concept of conservation to Marquis and his forebear, and was quite unaware of an approaching figure until footfalls intruded on the train of thought. Even then, there was a half-fantasy cross-over when the footsteps seemed to be appropriate enough to the gathering which had assembled in my mind. Perhaps Marquis arriving late, wandering up to the summit after an aid-free ascent of Pterodactyl on the Lost Valley Buttress?

Alas for my powers of summoning spirits, the voice which greeted me in relief that I was not a corpse (I suppose I had been sprawled and still for as long as I had been in his sight) spoke in the un-Gaelic vowels of Manchester, and belonged, as it quickly transpired, to a garrulous physicist who inhabited some nuclear hell-hole in the south. We agreed at once to differ about the merits of nuclear anythings, for the summit of a noble mountain is not a place to sully with such unworthiness when there are such things as comradeship and wilderness ideals to explore. Our differences paled then vanished for a while. He had diagnosed himself jaded, depressed and broke, and decided salvation lay in Glencoe, retiring after each day's climb to the back of a twenty-year-old Morris Minor van. He gestured at the mountains spilling away in the vague direction of Mull: "They haven't invented a drug that can revive you like this lot can."

I nodded, added that they have invented a drink which compliments it passably well, and we drank to the wilderness from my small emergency/hospitality supply of Talisker.

But I still had Collie and the others on my mind, and the fact that my new acquaintance had some difficulty with my accent brought me back to the scene I had devised. Collie is known to have found Marquis uncommunicative when they finally met around 1890, but the shepherd's fluency would have been in Gaelic and he had probably had little use for English for much of his life and felt awkward with it. I had, of course, contrived a common language for them for the purposes of my gathering of mountaineering spirits, and made the basic error of trying to let the nuclear one in on the proceedings. He had left within minutes, doubtless to regale his nuclear colleagues when he returned with stories of the mad, whisky-swilling Highlander he met on a mountain top, havering away about trysts with ghosts, and doubtless, by the time he was finished, I would be clad from head to toe in tartan and brandishing targe and broadsword. Still, we dwelt briefly on the same plane. I sat on and on, brewing tea from snow, watching mountain shadows shift. No other footfall, no wingbeat, no bird cry, no

"I sat on watching mountain shadows shift . . ."

stir of man or wind or weather intervened. Soon the physicist might never have been. I summoned no ghosts.

I slipped instead into a frame of mind which revelled in being alone, quite alone, in which every measured step down the ridge to the beallach and up to the summit of Stob Coire nan Lochan was relished for the simple fact that I was the only one in the world who heard its sound. I dared any moving silhouette to desecrate my skyline, defied any aircraft or eagle to trail its wake across my sky. None challenged me. The silence, in which I alone walked and breathed, was the ambassador of a powerful peace.

Down at the beallach again, I lingered over the last moments of the high mountain world, that upper chamber that you first glimpse from the road under Aonach Dubh. I reconstituted the day and let it fold into that scrapbook of the mind where we all store the golden hours. I stood by a long snow slope which led smoothly down into Coire Gabhail. I would glissade down in seconds, unreconciled to the act of descent. Marion Campbell knows such a moment. *Argyll - The Enduring Heartland* includes her poem "Levavi Oculus", the last two verses of which might have been written for here and now:

> But to come down again,
> To leave the holy ground and tread the earth,
> In from the brightness of infinity,
> Casting the lost glow of divinity
> Back to distress and dearth,
> Cramping beneath the burdens -
> God, the pain!

> Cry, for we left our Paradise today;
> But when we turn and load
> Accustomed burdens, grieving, if we say
> "None knows what we forego!"
> Then One says low,
> "I too, joyfully trod my hills and came away
> And bore a Burden up a stony road."

I too find my Burden-bearer among mountains. I would wander the cloisters of Coire Gabhail in the dusk and take the stony road home. Perhaps there would be ghosts in nailed boots for company.

The back-end of a Glasgow newspaper office night shift, a little after midnight, at which point the clock starts to slow down. Sundays were always the worst, and quiet Sundays the most excrutiatingly boring thing imaginable. A curious torpor overtakes the journalistic state of mind (which has trained and developed and honed its skills to react to things which *happen*) on those occasions when absolutely nothing at all happens. A conversation of quite pervasive lethargy was suddenly galvanised when it stumbled across the unsuspected common ground of mountains, and the stale, overheated air of that editorial floor became charged with the alpine tastes of high Glencoe, the salt winds of the Cuillins, the Arctic piledriver winds of the Cairngorms plateau. By 2a.m. we were well entrenched in that timeless, classless and endlessly intriguing tent and bothy and bivouac pastime of compiling lists of favourites. I delivered a short eulogy, a hymn of ecstatic praise, on Buachaille Etive Mór, somewhere in my top three (jousting with Bla-Bheinn and Braeriach), after which the conversation went:

"So you'll know the Rannoch Wall?"

"By sight, not to the touch. I'm not a hard rock wall man at heart."

"But you'll have done Curved Ridge then?" (This with the arched eyebrows and rising tone of voice which anticipated a barely credible negative response.)

"Ah, no, I told you, I'm not..."

"Yes, I heard you, a hard rock man at heart. Who says? Have you tried?"

"Scrambled a bit."

"How much?"

"A lot."

"Enjoy it?"

"Yes, but I ..." (the tormenting spectre of Ossian's Cave).

"Right, you and me for Curved Ridge. We're off work on Thursday, right? You'll love it."

"I delivered a short eulogy,
a hymn of ecstatic praise, on Buachaille Etive Mór . . ."

A handful of times in a mountaineering life, a day turns up to deflect the course of that life. It may be a deflection of millimetres or miles, but something of that day will colour every succeeding day for as long as mountains have a hold, however flimsy or fatal, on that life. One such day now dawned, early May and hot. Again the mountain was empty save for a solo climber racing up invisible routes on the Rannoch Wall like a ladybird on a bracken leaf. He was later diagnosed as a species of rock superstar with a number of hard new routes in the glen to his credit. He would join us for lunch halfway up Curved Ridge, and expressed some unspoken disappointment that we were a journeyman with apprentice in tow. He returned to his higher order of mountaineering like a small boy who has knocked on his neighbour's door and been told that his pal is not coming out to play. I paused to watch him often, admired the poise, the confident movement, the perfect balance - that of all things - which characterise all great mountaineers, the only time in my life I ever envied the high accomplished rock athlete his peculiar taste for confined freedom.

Curved Ridge is rock climbing for beginners, some exposure, a few problems to grapple, interspersed with little more than steep walks, a ragged staircase from which a few steps have gone missing to heighten the interest of the ascent. But it is a fundamental component in the Buachaille's rock architecture and leans close enough to all its framed arenas where man and nature joust for some of the mountain's matchless aura to rub off. It is also a highway through the history of mountaineering, for no-one who has carved a niche in that hall of fame has not climbed and blazed trails on the north-east face of the Buachaille from Collie onwards. Ken Crocket notes that fact in his guidebook, and adds a pointed footnote: "The Buachaille is more than just a concentration of good routes on rough rock - though this is undoubtedly true. It is also a living history of Scottish climbing, a long hard day in winter, a classic climb in the sun, a dismal retreat in the rain. If that were not sufficient praise for one mountain, its climbs look out over the Rannoch Moor - one of the last truly wild areas of Europe. All this should be treated gently and guarded fiercely."

So I treated Curved Ridge gently and with as little apprehension as I could, and under that sun and the competence of my guide, and in that mountain's bear-hugging embrace, I lost apprehension and became enthralled, a Murray for an hour. The spectre of Ossian's Cave was slain. I climbed more and more calmly, and have done so ever since, and although I never did graduate to Agag's Groove and other capillary ways up the mountain (I have always thirled to the silver wrinkles rather than the gray cliffs), I won the confidence to scramble eagerly, and learned to bless good rock. I also emerged under the Crowberry Tower a little more in awe of the Buachaille than before, my respect for it a little deeper, my affection for it boundless.

It is a short scramble from the Crowberry Gap to the summit of the Buachaille, and it was there that the expedition discovered that both it and the mountain were dry. We recalled flasks in the car, but neither of us could recall actually packing them. Resourcefulness has always been the stock-in-trade of newspapermen, however, and I rummaged deep and emerged with the small prerequisite hipflask of Talisker. It was at that point that we invented a new mountaineering sensation, and discovered that there are immense untapped commercial possibilities in a cocktail of Talisker and snow.

There is one further retrospective lesson learned from my first ascent of Curved Ridge, and one which has become a principle of my own mountain philosophy. It is that it is not enough to climb a mountain, to touch the cairn and pronounce it "climbed". Curved Ridge taught me that there is a heart to every mountain, a specific place, a collaboration of landscape circumstances, a rarified atmosphere - all or any of these things - which deepens perceptions of where you are, of why wildness matters. I have learned whenever, wherever I go among mountains, to seek out the mountain heart. It is not found at the first attempt, for such ready acquiescence is not in the nature of mountains. My first climb on Curved Ridge was my fifth ascent of the Buachaille; only then did I find a rhythmic unanimity with the mountain heartbeat. In all Glencoe, there is no higher prize.

Chapter Five
Primitive for All Time

THE 1952 EDITION of the Scottish Mountaineering Club Guide to the Central Highlands contains the following paragraph in its chapter entitled *"The Buachailles of Etive"* (the Italics are mine):

"The whole area now belongs to the National Trust for Scotland, who also own the Bidean nam Bian Group and the Aonach Eagach in Glencoe. The whole Trust property, about 13,000 acres (actually 14,200 acres now) is roughly a triangle with its three points at Dalness Lodge in Glen Etive, Clachaig Inn on the north-west, and Kinghouse Inn on the north-east. Free and unrestricted access to the mountains, corries and glens is permitted at all times, *and it is the intention of the Trust to preserve this beautiful mountain district in its present wild state and no roads, paths, cairns, or signposts will be allowed and no new building of any kind may be erected."*

That last presumption of the Trust's intentions may seem unduly naive now in light of the events of the intervening years and the policies which the Trust has brought to bear, but when it was written there was every good reason to make such a presumption, and no organisation more entitled to make it than the Scottish Mountaineering Club.

It was the SMC which, in a series of unprecendented fund-raising appeals through the mid 1930s, provided much of the money which brought the Glencoe lands into the ownership of the National Trust for Scotland. At the helm of the SMC's efforts was its president, Percy Unna, who used his contacts and his personal fortune (he donated - anonymously at the time - £5000 of the £6500 purchase price of the Dalness Estate) to secure the land for the Trust and therefore, the Scottish nation. But there were strings attached, and in those strings lies the basis of what has become one of the longest and most heated controversies of wild Scotland. It centres on the Trust's management of all its mountain properties (and Glencoe in particular, as it was the first), and its departure from what were established inside and outside the Trust as "The Unna Rules".

These "rules" were set out in a now celebrated letter from Unna as President of the SMC to the Chairman and Council of the National Trust for Scotland on November 23, 1937. It bears repeating in full:

Unna Country . . . Bidean towers above Achnambeitach

77

"Dear Sirs, - As the movement initiated by a group of members of the Scottish Mountaineering Club to acquire Dalness Forest and hand it over the the National Trust for Scotland, to be held for the use of the nation, so that the public may have unrestricted access at all times, has now materialised; as subscriptions to that end were invited not only from the members of the Scottish Mountaineering Club but also from the members of all other mountaineering clubs in Great Britain; and as the fund so subscribed enables the forest to be handed over free of cost to the Trust, together with a surplus to be used as an endowment fund - it is considered desirable that what are believed to be the view of the subscribers as to the future of the estate should be expressed in writing, and recorded in the minutes of the Trust. This is all the more necessary as in the attached circular which was issued for the purpose of inviting these subscriptions, it was stated that the land 'would be held on behalf of the public and preserved for their use,' and 'that the Trust' would 'be asked to undertake that the land be maintained in its primitive condition for all time with unrestricted access to the public.' The views in question are:

"1. That 'Primitive' means not less primitive than the existing state.

2. That sheep farming and cattle grazing may continue but that deer stalking must cease, and no sport of any kind be carried on, or sporting rights sold or let; any use of the property for sport being wholly incompatible with the intention that the public should have unrestricted access and use. It is understood, however, that deer may have to be shot, as that may be necessary to keep down numbers and so prevent damage, but for that purpose alone.

3. That the word 'unrestricted' does not exclude regulations, but implies that regulations, if any, should be limited to such as may be found absolutely necessary, and be in sympathy with the views expressed herein.

4. That the hills should not be made easier or safer to climb.

5. That no facilities should be introduced for mechanical transport; that paths should not be extended or improved; and that new paths should not be made.

6. That no directional or other signs, whether signposts, paintmarks, cairns or of any other kind whatsoever should be allowed: with the exception of such signs as

The glen and Loch Achtriochtan from the "silver wrinkles"

may be necessary to indicate that the land is the property of the Trust, and to give effect to the requirement in the Provisional Order of 1935 that by-laws must be exhibited.

7. That should a demand spring up for hotels or hostels, it is possible that it may have to be satisfied to a limited extent. If so, they should only be built alongside the public roads, and should be subject to control by the Trust; and it is suggested that no hotels or hostels should be built in Glencoe itself or any other part of the property, except, perhaps, in the lower reaches of the Trust property in Glen Etive. It is hoped that the Trust may be able to come to an understanding with neighbouring proprietors as to corresponding restrictions being maintained in regard to land near to that held by the Trust.

8. That no other facilities should be afforded for obtaining lodging, shelter, food or drink; and especially that no shelter of any kind be built on the hills.

9. It is hoped that the design of any buildings which may be necessary will be carefully considered by the Trust; and that where possible, trees will be planted in their vicinity.

10. In conclusion, it is suggested that the whole question of the management of Trust properties in Glen Etive and Glencoe should receive special attention, in view of the possibility that the policy adopted by the National Trust for Scotland in the present instance may create a precedent for similar areas in other mountainous districts, not only in Scotland, but also in England and Wales. - Yours faithfully, P. J. H. Unna."

These then are the Unna Rules, and for long enough they were accepted as the basis for management of National Trust for Scotland mountain properties, which were soon to include Kintail, Torridon, Ben Lawers and Goatfell on Arran. Unna made the Trust gifts of Kintail and Ben Lawers, an endowment fund for Torridon, and helped with the purchase of Goatfell and the Grey Mare's Tail waterfall in Dumfriesshire. By any standards it is a colossal debt which the Trust owes to Unna and his memory, yet so acute is the embarrassment which the Trust now feels over the Unna Rules controversy that in the 1986 edition of its own Glencoe guide,

Unna's name is not mentioned. It is, in the judgement of many climbers and conservationists, an unforgiveable sin of omission.

So what changed between that safe presumption in 1952 (the first edition of the SMC guide since the Trust had acquired Glencoe) and the present day when the Trust treats the Unna Rules as an albatross round its neck? What happened was that as people became generally more mobile in the late '50s and '60s, the Trust determined to increase visitor numbers, and therefore income, at all its properties, and publicised them accordingly. No distinction was made between the mountain properties and the other properties - the gardens, castles, houses and others - no recognition that increased visitor pressures would be destructive to the mountains. At Glencoe, aided and abetted by the Countryside Commission for Scotland, the Trust opened a new visitor centre in 1976. Tourism had already begun to invade the glen as never before, lured by new roadside car parking, and in 1966 a bridge across the Coe under Coire Gabhail, a new wooden staircase to reach the bridge, a new path connecting it to the roadside, and signposting to "The Lost Valley". The centre, the bridge, the paths, the signs and the car parks are all contrary to the Unna Rules. By that bridge now is a sign explaining a policy of woodland regeneration which will conceal the "footpath scar" from the road. That scar is a landscape wound inflicted by Trust policy, a policy which the Unna Rules forbid. The explanatory sign itself is against the rules.

Murray wrote in 1947 of wading the Coe "whose fifteen mile length bars access to the mountain and helps to preserve the Lost Valley's sanctity. We went down to the river's bank. It was sullied by no bridge hereabouts and we were faced with a knee-deep wade of twenty yards . . ."

"Spring or autumn" wrote Murray, ". . . a man might come here for a week and be alone. He might pitch a tent on that meadow and be as much out of sight and sound of civilisation as if he dwelt at the North Pole . . ." No more.

Other features of the glen were signposted. The passes of the Lairig Gartain and Lairig Eilde were cairned. Hordes of boots and Glencoe's climate did the rest.

Unna's Rules were breached to one extent or another at every mountain property the Trust owned, and at Ben Lawer's, Unna's personal gift, another visitor centre and

Sunlight contrives many shades and subtleties
amid the glen's lower slopes

vast car park were built high on the mountain, the path cairned (with paint splashed rocks for a while) all the way to the summit, and in an act of supreme insensitivity which would have outraged Unna, a memorial to him was put on the summit.

The Trust has since retreated from some of the worst excesses of such policies in the face of years of criticism. Publicity has in some cases been toned down, some of the signposting has gone, but not the bridges, not the visitor centres, not the car parks, not the central policy which insists Unna's Rules are negotiable. An article in the Trust's own magazine, Heritage Scotland, in the summer of 1987, reflects current Trust thinking on Unna:

"He set out valuable guidelines (but not conditions) for the administration of the mountains he helped to buy for the Trust, which the Trust have striven to uphold in the spirit of what they think Unna would have approved of 50 years on, and in the light of the greatly increased numbers of people who now wish to enjoy the hills and the countryside."

I have a certain sympathy for the Trust's dilemma. Firstly it is no easy task administering a place like Glencoe, and remember it is just one of many diverse and important properties for which it is responsible. Secondly, the Unna Rules are not easy to live up to, and their uncompromising nature will only make them harder to live up to as pressures on wild land increase. Thirdly, there *are* greater pressures on our mountain heartlands than ever before, and reconciling these with the needs of wild landscape is a formidable task. The fact is, however, that the only real dilemma facing the Trust is whether or not it is up to that formidable task. The Unna Rules exist. They are a fact. They are not "guidelines" they are conditions, rules. Official documents and correspondence and conversation within and outwith the Trust referred to 'rules' or 'conditions', certainly well into the seventies. When the SMC referred to the purchase of Kintail in its 1945 journal, it said that "one of the conditions of the gift was that it should be administered in accordance with the general principles expressed by the members of the Scottish Mountaineering Club at the time when Dalness was acquired by the Trust". It is only recently that the Trust has begun to insinuate "guidelines" and other watered down substitutes into the debate.

The Trust has spawned its own monster in Glencoe. Many of its most flagrant breaches of the Unna Rules are attempts to control or otherwise cater for the excessive numbers of people it has encouraged, damage limitation on the grand scale.

But what the National Trust for Scotland has found hardest to live up to throughout the debate, is a passage of five sentences in its own official publication, "The National Trust for Scotland Guide". They come from the Trust's president, the Earl of Wemyss and March:

"Behind the munificence of this remarkable man (Unna) there is a simple motive. He appreciated, as few others did in the 1930s, that we have in the Highlands of Scotland one of the last large reserves of wild and semi-wild land in Europe. He apprehended a threat which is now a stark reality - intolerable pressure on areas which are easy of access to a motorized population - and determined that so far as his resources and the wit of the Trust could provide for protection and temperate use, the high places would remain for the pleasure and refreshment of the man on foot . . ." Those were the first three sentences. They accurately identify Unna's motive, they acknowledge his vision as a prophetic one - there were no real pressures on wild land in the 1930s when he acted so decisively. They acknowledge the priorities of "protection and temperate use" since when protection has all but vanished and use has been encouraged along far from temperate lines. Then there are the last two sentences of this summary of Unna's importance to the Trust:

"The Unna Rules' which he formulated some time before his death in 1950 have a spartan simplicity. I pray that we shall be able to abide by them."

Alas for the power of prayer, that book was published in 1976, the same year in which the Trust opened its Glencoe Visitor Centre, a floodgate through which intemperate use poured and continues to pour. It also marked the point at which the first commandment of the Unna doctrine was laid to rest . . . "that the Trust be asked to undertake that the land be maintained in its primitive condition for all time . . . that 'primitive' means not less primitive than the existing state . . ."

Neither the letter nor the spirit of Unna have been upheld in Glencoe. The Unna Rules, by that very "spartan simplicity" are so unambiguous that they are not

A landscape and a philosophy of "spartan simplicity"
"...primitive for all time..."

open to interpretation. If he had insisted on nothing other than that the land be maintained in its primitive condition for all time, today's Trust policies would be no less at variance with his wishes.

It should be remembered too that Unna had such confidence in the Trust in 1937, that he asked them to set such an example that neighbouring landowners and other mountain estates all over Britain would follow suit. The example which *has* been set is not one to emulate, and the standard which Unna flew for the wilderness is in tatters.

Unna's cause is not completely lost, however. He has growing battalions of disciples and many well-known champions among mountaineers and conservationists. New generations are discovering him and the spartan simplicity of his philosophy, and asking how the practice has become so removed from the theory. Criticism of Trust management in Glencoe and elsewhere has become more and more public, the Unna Rules a source of ever greater sensitivity to Trust staff, council, and rank-and-file members. I believe the Trust *is* bound by the Unna Rules, and that the more difficult it becomes to implement them, the more important it becomes to implement them scrupulously. It will only happen, however, if conservationists and mountaineers in Scotland and beyond unite behind Unna's standard, in a sustained campaign for a return within Trust management to those simple, spartan values he demanded.

It may take some time before the visitor centre is demolished, before tourism is relegated to a lower priority than the mountain landscape, before the mountains are restored to their primitive state; but the removal of the "Lost Valley bridge" over the Coe and the paths and car parks which service it are surely achievable targets of no little symbolism for Unna's standard bearers.

There *are* new standard bearers for Unna. Their motive is not anti-Trust but pro-landscape. Their motive is his motive. Protection and temperate use of the landscape is not a bad ambition, as long as anybody's definition of "temperate" is coloured by that first of all Unna's commandments - primitive, for all time.

". . . a MacDiarmid of a mountain . . ."

Chapter Six
Homage to the Herdsman

THE MOUNTAIN is in shadow. No sun alights on the Herdsman's plaid, although it jigged and reeled about Sron na Creise and Meall a' Bhuiridh for one dancing morning hour. Now in mid-January's noon, the year's first snow illuminates the Herdsman, swaddles the mountain in fleeces.

All morning I have walked or stood or sat by the Herdsman's feet throwing idolatrous glances, gazes, staring out faces I find in the ceaseless rearrangements of rock and snow. Sometimes, in certain alignments of cloud it wears - sideways - the torn shape of Scotland.

That's it. The mountain stands for the shadowed and torn Scotland I believe in. It is not a Munro of a mountain or a Corbett, or any other species of ticked off and tabled mountain because it is so unclassifiably unique. It's a MacDiarmid of a mountain!

> - This terrible blinding discovery
> Of Scotland in me, and I in Scotland

I walk out to the mountain as I might have walked out to greet Hugh MacDiarmid, with a lump the size of Crowberry Tower in my throat. To be a Scot and stand under Buachaille Etive Mór is to rejoice that whatever the flaws in the land, however it is shadowed and torn, the spirit of its singular Highland landscape is encapsulated in this singular mountain, ward of the Great Herdsman. "All this should be treated gently and guarded fiercely."

If some as yet unmasked deity of Glencoe should suddenly rise to the landscape's defence (having seen all that has shadowed and torn Glencoe through its countless eras) and curtail my wandering instincts to a single mile, I would plead for half that - the bank of the Coupall from below Jacksonville to just above Etive, and back, so that however I plied that folded mile, the mountain would be forever ahead or over my shoulder. I would plead, too, for a Coupall well fed and fired up by a winter month of spates and snows. That way, with the river unfordable and my allocation of its bank "sullied by no bridge", I could set the mountain at an untouchable distance, symbolic of wilderness.

". . . I would feel its crouching presence at my back . . ."

91

Each time I walked north, I would lock my gaze into the mountain's pyramidical perfection, ingrain its form in every light and shadow and weather on my mind's eye, so that wherever other wanderings might lead, I could recall the Herdsman's aura by blinking. Each time I walked south, towards Etive, I would feel its crouching presence at my back, so that time and again I would turn and startle again at the MacDiarmid-ness of its art.

> . . . and the principal question
> Aboot a work o' art is frae hoo deep
> A life it springs - and syne hoo faur
> Up frae't it has the poo'er to leap.

How long does it take to sculpt such a mountain, to energise such a power and such a leap up from the shoreline of that moor-sea called Rannoch? As long, perhaps, as a land incubates the embryo of its language then gives it birth, then nurtures it until it pronounces itself ready to unleash a mountainous poet, a MacDiarmid, on its landscape.

But here, under Buachaille Etive Mór, threshold of all Glencoe, gathered in by the Great Herdsman, it is the Scotland in me which overflows, a love not totally unrequited for a mountain land.

Paul Cezanne said: "What art is primarily about is what the eye thinks." His eye thought so much of one mountain, Mont St. Victoire at Aix-en-Provence, he thought it worth painting again and again forever, the mountain growing in stature and abstraction the more he painted it, the more his eye thought about it. My eye thinks much the same where I sit under Buachaille Etive Mór, studious and seduced. It is a mountain to satisfy a Cezanne. Circumnavigate the Buachaille, shape and re-shape it, build and re-build all its landforms, let your eye paint its every profile again and again forever until it is a familiarity you crave, until you must breathe the Buachaille, not air. Know then what love impelled in Cezanne, intimately alone with *his* mountain, what Buachailles we'd have seen if only Glencoe had a climate like Aix-en-Provence!

Buachaille Etive Mór ... "a mountain to satisfy a Cezanne"

If love is
a perfect exchange of souls
my love is a mountain.

If love is
the embrace of unfailing arms
my love is the corrie of the mountain.

If love is
a song under stars
my love is the mountain of the night.

If love is
tranquil in turmoil
silent in trust
rock in shifting sand
my love is the unfailing mountain.

If love is
eagle-loyal
lichen-tenacious
berry-bright
my love is the living mountain.

If love is
true
if love is
forever
if love is

my love is the eternal mountain.

Selected Bibliography

Campbell, Marion — *Argyll, The Enduring Heartland*, Turnstone Press, 1977

Crocket, Ken — *Glencoe and Glen Etive Rock and Ice Climbs Guide*, Scottish Mountaineering Trust, 1980

Gordon, Seton — *Highways and Byways in the West Highlands*, MacMillan, 1935

Hugo, Richard — *The Right Madness on Skye*, W. W. Norton, New York, 1980

MacDiarmid, Hugh — *The Hugh MacDiarmid Anthology*, Routledge and Kegan Paul, 1972

Morton, H.V. — *In Search of Scotland*, Methuen, 1929

Murray, Sarah — *A Companion and Useful Guide to The Beauties of Scotland*, first published 1799, now Byways Books, 1982.

Murray, W.H. — *Mountaineering in Scotland, 1947*, and *Undiscovered Scotland, 1951*, both Dent

Naismith, Robert J. — *Buildings of the Scottish Countryside*, Victor Gollancz, 1985

National Trust for Scotland — *Glencoe*, Marketing Services Division

National Trust for Scotland — *The National Trust for Scotland Guide*, Jonathan Cape, 1976

Prebble, John — *The Lion in the North, 1971*, and *Glencoe, 1966*, both Penguin

Scottish Mountaineering Club — *The Central Highlands*, 1952

Information

Glencoe lies wholly in the old Scottish county of Argyllshire, although it is now technically a part of Strathclyde Region. Much of the glen – about 14,000 acres – is owned by the National Trust for Scotland. The highest point is the summit of Bidean nam Bian which at 3766 feet (1148 metres) is also the highest point in Argyll. A reputation for high rainfall and low cloud often makes navigation difficult and accidents are frequent. Good equipment, an appropriate map (O.S. Sheet 41 or Tourist Map for Ben Nevis and Glencoe), and a thorough apprenticeship on lesser hills and mountains are thoroughly recommended.